NOOK Tablet™
FOR
DUMMIES®
PORTABLE EDITION

NOOK Tablet™
FOR
DUMMIES®
Portable Edition

by Corey Sandler

WILEY

John Wiley & Sons, Inc.

NOOK Tablet™ For Dummies® Portable Edition

Published by
John Wiley & Sons, Inc.
111 River Street
Hoboken, NJ 07030-5774

www.wiley.com

Copyright © 2012 by John Wiley & Sons, Inc., Hoboken, New Jersey

Published by John Wiley & Sons, Inc., Hoboken, New Jersey

Published simultaneously in Canada

WILEY

About the Author

Corey Sandler is a voracious reader and an indefatigable author: books, magazine pieces and, ages ago, newspapers. He has written more than nearly 200 books at last count, about computers and technology, history, sports, and business. When he's not at the keyboard, Sandler travels all over the world as a lecturer aboard luxury cruise ships. (Someone has to do it.)

Okay, so sometimes he is fatigable. That happens when you carry 150 pounds of luggage including a laptop, two tablets, three cameras, four lenses, five electrical plugs, half a dozen books to read and consult, and a hogshead of lecture notes printed out and neatly bound to sit on a lectern. And that's one major reason why he's a fan of electronic books. It's good for his back.

Sandler studied journalism at Syracuse University; he also took some courses to learn how to program a gigantic IBM mainframe computer and worked nights at a newspaper printing plant.

He began his career as a daily newspaper reporter in Ohio and then New York, moving on to a post as a correspondent for Associated Press. From there he joined Ziff-Davis Publishing as the first executive editor of *PC Magazine*. He wrote his first book about computers in 1983 and hasn't come close to stopping. When he's not out to sea or in a foreign country and living on his smartphone, tablet, and computer, he's at home on Nantucket Island 30 miles off the coast of Massachusetts. He shares his life with his wife Janice; two grown children have their own careers elsewhere on the continent.

You can see Sandler's current list of books on his web site at www.sandlerbooks.com and send an e-mail through the links you find there. He promises to respond to courteous inquiries as quickly as he can. Spam, on the other hand, will receive the death penalty.

Dedication

This book is dedicated to my home team. Janice has put up with me for more than 30 years and still laughs at most of my jokes. My children, William and Tessa, are no longer constantly underfoot, embarked now on careers of their own, but when I need consultation on social networks and cultural references beyond the scope of Old Dad, they're the first to text, IM, or tweet.

Author's Acknowledgments

This book bears just one name on the cover, but that's only part of the story.

Thanks to the smart and capable crew at Wiley, including Katie Mohr and the rest of the editorial and production staff, who turned the taps of my keyboard into the book you hold in the electronic device in the palm of your hand.

Also, my appreciation to long-time publishing collaborator Tonya Maddox Cupp, who once again managed the process with grace and humor.

And as always, thanks to you for buying this book. Go forth and enjoy your NOOK Tablet for escapades on the World Wide Web, audio, video, games, and easy (and weightless) access to millions of great works of literature, thoughtful history and analysis, and humble heapings of help like the very one you are reading now.

Publisher's Acknowledgments

We're proud of this book; please send us your comments at http://dummies.custhelp. com. For other comments, please contact our Customer Care Department within the U.S. at 877-762-2974, outside the U.S. at 317-572-3993, or fax 317-572-4002.

Some of the people who helped bring this book to market include the following:

Acquisitions and Editorial

Project Editor: Tonya Maddox Cupp

Senior Acquisitions Editor: Katie Mohr

Editorial Manager: Jodi Jensen

Editorial Assistant: Amanda Graham

Sr. Editorial Assistant: Cherie Case

Cover Photo: ©iStockphoto.com / BanksPhotos

Cartoons: Rich Tennant (www.the5thwave.com)

Composition Services

Project Coordinator: Kristie Rees

Layout and Graphics: Claudia Bell

Proofreaders: Laura Albert, Debbye Butler, Jessica Kramer

Indexer: Potomac Indexing, LLC

Publishing and Editorial for Technology Dummies

 Richard Swadley, Vice President and Executive Group Publisher

 Andy Cummings, Vice President and Publisher

 Mary Bednarek, Executive Acquisitions Director

 Mary C. Corder, Editorial Director

Publishing for Consumer Dummies

 Kathleen Nebenhaus, Vice President and Executive Publisher

Composition Services

 Debbie Stailey, Director of Composition Services

Table of Contents

Introduction

*W*hat *is* a NOOK Tablet?

Depending upon how you look at it, it's one of these:

- An eBook eReader that adds many (but not all) of the features of a tablet computer, including a wireless Internet connection and an audio and video player.
- A tablet computer (somewhat limited in its features) with a bright, colorful screen that you can use to read eBooks.

Before I talk about the limitations, let me crow about the abilities of the NOOK Tablet. In a small and highly portable plastic case, you will find the following:

- A high-resolution backlit LCD screen, capable of displaying crisp text in a book, magazine, a newspaper, or other document. A few minutes into reading the latest bestseller or a classic of literature and you'll completely forget that there's no ink or paper involved.
- Spectacular color graphics, perfect for reading magazines, comics, or children's books. Just as an example, if you love *National Geographic* or *Sports Illustrated* or *Vanity Fair* in their print editions, you'll be blown away with their electronic versions.
- Built into the screen: the ability to sense your touch. When you need a keyboard, one appears. You can also swipe, flick, pinch, and otherwise rule your domain by hand.
- An eReader for documents created on computers, including word processors, Excel spreadsheets, and basic PowerPoint presentations. It can read PDF files.
- A full-featured browser allows you to visit any page on the web and shop for shoes, read the news, get the blues, and just about whatever else you do in cyberspace. The Internet connection flows both ways: You can buy books

and magazines, and you can put aside the eBook to do a bit of research on your own.

- Built-in facilities to read and write e-mail using nearly all major e-mail providers.

- Electronic piping that streams videos: from YouTube, news pages, or from sites that deliver (sometimes free, sometimes for a fee) TV shows and movies.

- A jukebox in a tablet, able to play music you've bought from online sites as well as tunes you already own and have transferred from a desktop or laptop computer.

- An art gallery in your hands, capable of storing and displaying photos and videos you've taken with a digital camera or collected from other sources.

- A game room where you never have to pick up the pieces, including chess, crossword puzzles, and Sudoku.

- Apps (productivity, game, information, and others) you can get — usually for a small fee — from the Barnes and Noble online store.

I did promise to mention the limitations of the NOOK Tablet, so here goes:

- There's no camera.

- Bluetooth communication isn't available (in the initial release of the hardware).

- You'll have to get around without GPS.

- You can't put an image on a separate video screen (such as a big screen TV).

- And — at least at the start — Barnes and Noble plans to keep tight control over the apps. So, while the iPad, Android, and other app stores swell with new products daily, B&N will keep its focus on products related to bookselling.

Foolish Assumptions

I assume that you have a NOOK Tablet. I also assume that you have access to the Internet using WiFi in your home or office, and that you can get around on the Internet. And I fervently believe you have (or can use) a personal computer or laptop computer so you can transfer files using the USB cable that came with your NOOK Tablet.

Icons Used in This Book

NOOK Tablet For Dummies uses certain art to get your attention.

You could hurt yourself, your machine, or your identity by not following these instructions.

Don't forget.

Let me save you some time, money, or heartache.

Pardon the interruption, but here's a bit of explanation for those of you who want to understand the why as well as the how.

Where to Go from Here

You go just about anywhere you want, of course. You go out of the house and take your book collection and web browser and music and videos with you. You go on planes, trains, and automobiles (as long as you're not the pilot, engineer, or driver). You don't go into the shower or the steam room.

Chapter 1

Getting to NOOK You . . .

*I*n the beginning, there were books. And they were nicely bound between hard covers. Then came paperbacks, which were smaller and portable. They could go with you on trips. But a stack of ten was a heavy load. And engineers built a computer. Then the computers became laptops and were small enough to carry around. Soon, scientists created the eReader. It was a clever thing — a device about the size of a pamphlet that could hold thousands of books. Then came tablets. By its evolving definition, a *tablet* has many computer capabilities centered around a touch-sensitive, full-color display that supplies its own lighting.

And one other thing: The NOOK Tablet is a close cousin to an earlier device from Barnes & Noble, the NOOKcolor. The differences are subtle but important. The NOOK Tablet is faster, smarter, has more built-in storage, and boasts an enhanced operating system. They're both fine devices, but in my opinion the NOOKcolor is an eReader with a touch of multipurpose communications capability, and the NOOK Tablet is an entry-level tablet that is also quite good as an eReader.

Inspecting the Gadget

When you need to enter characters or numbers (to move around the web, type in an e-mail address, or the like), a virtual keyboard will appear onscreen. When it does, you can tap away at the touchscreen. It isn't difficult to use, but I don't want you to get the idea that you can easily use the NOOK Tablet to write the Great American Novel. You can read *The Adventures of Huckleberry Finn* or *The Great Gatsby* with ease and style. When you're ready to write your own masterpiece, I recommend a computer with a physical keyboard and a large screen. See Figure 1-1.

Hold on to the box that your NOOK Tablet came in. If you need to send in the device for warranty service, this is premade packaging for the purpose. And if you choose to someday regift your tablet to someone else and upgrade to the next wondrous model, it will look so much more impressive if it arrives in its original packaging.

All of the following descriptions are based on looking at the NOOK Tablet lying on its back, with its top facing away from you and the bottom closest to you: very much like the way you would look at a page from a book.

The front

The front is home to just three items of note, two of them quite important and one strictly for whimsy:

- ✔ VividView Color Touchscreen
- ✔ The Home button: ∩
- ✔ The NOOK notch: strictly for whimsy

Figure 1-1: The screen comes up when you need it.

See Figure 1-2 for a guided tour.

Power button   Touchscreen   Headphone jack

Microphone   Volume buttons

microSD memory card slot   microUSB port   Home button

Figure 1-2: The essential buttons, ports, and slots.

VividView Color Touchscreen

Barnes & Noble calls the technology for its color touchscreen VividView. That means, obviously, that they feel the tablet offers a view that's quite vivid, and in that they're quite correct. There are a few other details worth noting: The screen employs something called *in-plane switching (IPS)*. IPS is an improved version of the LCD that offers wider viewing angles and better color reproduction than earlier designs. The NOOK laminates the display to the surface of the touchscreen, which reduces reflection and glare. The touchscreen uses capacitive sensing, meaning that it detects the precise location of your touch as your finger disrupts the display's electrostatic field. I thought you'd get a charge out of that.

Home button

The Home button is marked with the NOOK symbol, which looks like this: ∩. If your NOOK Tablet is *sleeping* — with its screen turned off to reduce battery use — the screen is also locked so that accidental touches don't perform actions. Touch the Home button to wake up the device and turn on the screen.

If the screen is already awake, touching the ∩ button takes you back to the Home screen. If you have told the system to require a password to start or reawaken, you will have to enter the four-digit secret code. Once you do that, the NOOK Tablet returns to the screen you were on before it went to dreamland.

If you don't make the NOOK Tablet require a password, you'll need to give the reader a special little wake-up swipe. The sleeping device will display a white ∩ in a green circle near the lower-left corner of the screen. Press the green circle and drag it to the right to unlock the device and return to the last screen you were viewing.

NOOK notch

The NOOK Tablet, like its older cousin the NOOKcolor, has a cute little open notch in the lower-left corner. It looks for all the world like a place to hang something — perhaps a mountaineer's carabiner. But please don't. The designers who worked with Barnes & Noble wanted to make their reader immediately recognizable from across the room and this was the artistic element they came up with.

However, don't use the NOOK notch to hook the NOOK Tablet to your belt buckle (or to anything else). Although I'm sure some people will think it's cute to attach a rabbit's foot to the notch, let me join with B&N in recommending against it: You just might end up damaging the screen.

The top and the right

Amazingly, the right is just like the left, only on the other side. Here you find the + and – volume buttons. I know you could figure this out, but here goes anyway: + means raise the volume and – means turn it down. The tablet doesn't go to 11.

The top has a headphone socket where you can plug in earbuds.

The bottom

There's not much to look at down here, except for one important entry point: a microUSB port. This connector serves two purposes:

- ✓ Through this port the USB cable that came with your tablet attaches to the AC adapter, allowing you to recharge the internal battery.

- ✓ You can use the USB cable to connect the NOOK Tablet to a computer to transfer files (a *side-load* in techno-speak). You can drag and drop any PDF or EPUB files from other sources, as well as compatible files from word processors, spreadsheets, and presentation programs. You can also move files from the tablet to your computer.

If you're comfortable with the basic operations of a Windows or Macintosh computer, you can attach your NOOK Tablet and allow it to be recognized as a storage device — essentially the same as an external hard drive or a flash memory key. You can also connect to a digital book manager like Adobe Digital Editions or calibre to manage files. (I explain book buying and file transfer in Chapter 3.)

The left

Here you find a powerful button. In fact, it is so powerful and so important that it's all by itself. It is, in fact, the power button.

- ✔ **To turn it on:** Press and hold the silver button for 3 or 4 seconds (One Mississippi, two Mississippi . . .) and release it to turn it on. If your tablet needs a password, enter that four-digit number.

- ✔ **To turn it off:** Press and hold the little rectangular button for about three or four seconds. (One Mississippi, two Mississippi . . .). A message asks if you really, really want to do that; tap the Power Off button to confirm.

The NOOK Tablet's electronic instruction manual (at the end of 2011, anyway) says to press and hold the power button for 2, 3, or 5 seconds to turn on or off the tablet. It makes you kind of think the manual was written by a committee. I've chosen an average: 3 to 4 seconds should do the trick.

You don't have to turn off your NOOK Tablet when you're through using it. It can tell that you haven't tapped its screen for a few minutes. It will turn off its LCD screen and go to sleep. Or, press and immediately release the power button to send it to Sleep mode. The advantage is that when you wake the NOOK Tablet, it jumps right back to where you were the last time you were paying attention to it.

If you start with a fully charged battery and let it go to sleep, the NOOK Tablet should sleep for several weeks. (Make sure the WiFi radio is turned off, or the battery will drain even while the tablet is sleeping.)

Why would you want to completely turn off the NOOK Tablet?

✔ You're on an airplane that's taking off or landing.

✔ You're in a hospital or the like.

✔ You want to put your tablet on the shelf for a month while you sit down to write your own Great American (or Canadian) Novel.

The back

The tablet's back has two important bits of business, and they're shown in Figure 1-3.

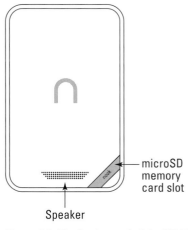

— microSD memory card slot

Speaker

Figure 1-3: The back panel of the NOOK Tablet is the source of sound and expanded memory.

The speaker

Near the USB port is a small speaker. Don't expect the sound quality (or volume) to rival your stereo system. The audio is good enough to hear system notification tones and — with a bit of effort — music or audio. But if you plan to groove to some of your personal tunes, buy earbuds and plug them into the outlet at the top end. If you want to share the sound with someone, you can buy a splitter that allows two devices to plug into the same jack.

If you're going to be listening to music or speech, it may help if you do not lay the tablet flat on its back; to get the best sound, the speaker should not be covered.

The microSD Slot (microSDHC Slot)

This tiny opening (just above the artistic-but-not-intended-to-hold-a-carabiner open space) can accept a little sliver of electronic flash memory (called a *microSD* or *microSDHC card*) as large as 32GB. This card holds information that is in addition to your tablet's built-in memory. And though 32GB is a whole lot of room, if you fill up one card, simply remove it and install a new card. See Figure 1-4.

Figure 1-4: This 32GB microSDHC card is from Kingston Technology.

Getting More Bits on SD or SDHC

SD and SDHC are known as *flash memory.* That means once data is recorded, it remains in place even when the power is turned off.

The tablet's instruction manual and some advertising are a bit imprecise in the description of the type of memory card. Here are the facts:

- ✔ *Do* buy a microSD or microSDHC card.
- ✔ *Don't* buy an SD or miniSD card.
- ✔ *Don't* buy a microSDXC card.

I recommend buying a card with these specs:

- ✔ microSDHC card
- ✔ 16GB or 32GB
- ✔ Class 6 speed
- ✔ Made by Kingston, Lexar, Sandisk, or Transcend

Installing a microSD or microSDHC card

The kind designers of the NOOK Tablet made sure you don't need a post-graduate degree in engineering to install a memory card. You can get to the card slot without removing the back cover; you need no tools other than your fingers.

Just take your time, be careful, and follow these instructions to install a memory card:

1. Turn off the device.

Technically this isn't required, but it is a good practice anytime you're working with electrical devices.

2. **Cover a well-lit, clean, level surface with a soft cloth. Lay the reader face down on the cloth.**

   Make sure there are no cups of coffee, soda, water, molten iron, or anything else that could spill onto your tablet.

3. **Find the small gray protective cover near the open curved corner. Using the tip of your finger, gently pull the lip open and fold it flat against the back of the device.**

4. **Hold the memory card *with the logo facing up toward you;* carefully slide it into the slot.**

   Push gently against the card until it's fully in place. See Figure 1-5. Don't force it into place; if you have the correct memory card (a microSD or microSDHC), it should fit easily. If it looks about twice as large as the opening, you've got the wrong card. Micros only need apply.

5. **Close the small gray lid and snap it into place.**

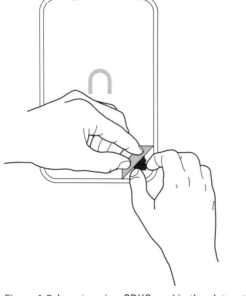

Figure 1-5: Insert a microSDHC card in the slot on the back.

To remove a memory card from your tablet, follow the first three steps for installing a card and then carefully slide the card out of its slot. Place the card in the protective case it came in (or in a clean plastic bag) and put it away for future use. Close the small gray lid and snap it into place.

Formatting a microSD or microSDHC

Your new microSDHC card may come *formatted* (a process that electronically indexes its memory so that the computer inside your tablet knows where to store or retrieve information). If you install an unformatted microSD or microSDHC card, the NOOK Tablet shows you a warning. No biggie: Use the Format command.

To format a microSD or microSDHC memory card from the warning, follow these steps:

1. **Tap the Format Now button.**

   You're asked if you are sure. Sure you're sure!

2. **Tap Format Now.**

Babying the Battery

To do all the gee-whiz things, your NOOK Tablet needs electrical power. Specifically, it needs a properly charged battery; the good news is that the device's lithium ion battery is rechargeable.

Chances are your new NOOK Tablet will arrive with not much of a charge in its electrical tank. And therefore, the first thing you want to do — after you open the box — is plug it in and put some juice in the battery. If you are really, really determined (impatient?) to try your new tablet as soon as it arrives, go ahead and turn on the power; if there's not enough of a charge, the NOOK Tablet will either refuse to start or display a warning message along these lines: *Get thee to a chargery.*

If you turn on your NOOK Tablet when its battery is almost gone, you get a warning to begin recharging before you try to use the tablet. If the battery is depleted, the tablet will shut down until it has been sufficiently recharged.

Charging checklist:

✔ The only officially sanctioned source of power for your NOOK Tablet is the AC adapter provided by Barnes & Noble. (It's the same adapter that the NOOKcolor uses.) Although there's nothing special about the adapter, the USB cable provided for the charger isn't standard.

✔ However: You *may* be able to find a replacement AC charger and cable with identical specifications from a third party; check and double-check before using one.

✔ You can buy a car charger from B&N.

✔ You can't charge the NOOK Tablet using the power output of a USB port on a personal computer or laptop.

Getting power from the wall

The NOOK Tablet AC adapter is a small cube that plugs into a wall outlet or power strip. To use it, you also need to attach the microUSB cable to the cube at one end and to your tablet at the other. See Figure 1-6.

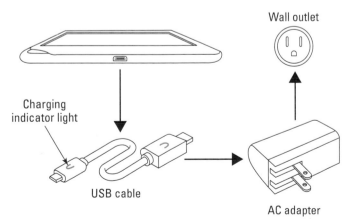

Wall outlet

Charging
indicator light

USB cable

AC adapter

Figure 1-6: The power adapter and its detachable USB cable look like this.

Reading the blog entries on the Barnes & Noble website, it is apparent that more than a few owners of the original NOOKcolor felt that the construction AC adapter was lacking. The adapter and its cable are covered under the standard one-year warranty for the NOOK Tablet. If you have trouble in that first year, get in touch with customer care and politely insist on a replacement unit.

Follow these steps to charge up:

1. **Plug the large end of the USB cable into the right spot on the AC adapter.**

2. **Plug the small end of the USB cable into your NOOK Tablet.**

3. **Plug the power adapter into a compatible electrical wall outlet or power strip.**

   The adapter can work with power between 110 to 240 volts; however, the plug is for use in the United States and Canada. You *can* connect your NOOK Tablet power adapter to a *plug adapter,* which would let you plug into a European or other foreign power source that uses a different plug shape. (There are a lot of *plugs* and *adapters* in this paragraph; re-read it carefully if you're going to travel outside the United States or Canada. Otherwise, press on with this chapter.)

   If your NOOK Tablet was turned off, it will turn itself on. The charging indicator light on the special USB cable lights up with an orange ∩ symbol (at the port where it connects to the tablet). Depending on how much power remains in the battery, it might take as many as 4 hours to fully recharge your device; when the work is done the ∩ symbol on the cable turns green with gratitude.

Don't turn off the NOOK Tablet while it's charging.

Locking or unlocking the tablet

When you allow (or command) your NOOK Tablet to go to sleep, the screen shuts off to save power. It also locks the touchscreen so you can't accidentally touch or swipe and make it do something.

To wake your NOOK from a doze, do this:

1. **Press the ∩ button at the bottom of the front side of the tablet.**

2. **If you have a password:** Tap the virtual number pad to provide the secret code.

   If you don't have a password: Press the green circle (near the bottom end of the screen) and drag it to the right. I explain touchscreen gestures in the next chapter.

   Once you unlock the NOOK Tablet using either method, you're back to the last screen you were before.

Chapter 2

Poking Around at Settings

*T*he NOOK Tablet's tappable, swipable, scrollable touch-screen allows you to truly enter the virtual world. You can tap a picture of a book cover to read or buy it. You can flick your way through web pages with your pointing finger. You can swipe from left to right (or vice versa) to slide through menus. And you can scroll up or down on a list of options.

Keeping the Gestures Polite

I'm not talking about using your hands or fingers in a particular way to express your opinion of a great work of literature or the latest piece of pointless piffle by a pompous politician. The gestures are pretty easy to master, and essential. You've got no choice: They've taken away your keyboard, mouse, fountain pen, stylus, and chisel.

Here is the basic set of gestures; not every page offers the same set of features, but you'll quickly learn how to tap-dance your way anywhere you want to go.

Tap

A *tap* is a quick strike by the tip of your finger. Think of poking at a key on a computer keyboard.

Double tap

Bet you figured this one out, right? A *double tap* is two pokes by the tip of your finger in quick succession.

- ✔ Double-tapping the Home screen cleans things up and arranges book and periodical covers in a grid.

- ✔ If you're at the Home screen, Daily Shelf, or Library, double-tapping a book cover displays details about the item. You get the same result double-tapping a book cover in the B&N online bookstore.

- ✔ On the web or in the picture gallery, double-tapping an image zooms you in. The same happens when you're reading a PDF file, including some books that are stored in that format.

- ✔ Double-tapping an enlarged image or page from a PDF will return the image or page to its original size.

Press and hold

Touch a finger to the screen and hold it there for 2 seconds. Oh, and then lift your finger off the screen; your finger doesn't have to become a permanent part of your NOOK Tablet. See Figure 2-1. On some other tablets and smartphones, the press-and-hold gesture is called a *long press*.

Depending on what's onscreen, a press-and-hold usually opens a menu.

- ✔ Press and hold a book cover and then release to show a menu with options such as Open the Book, Recommend It, or Lend It.

- ✔ Press and hold on an item on the Daily Shelf to get the opportunity to remove the book from display.

- ✔ Press and hold, then lift, from a word in a book to open the Text Selection Toolbar. This particular menu lets you look up a word in the NOOK Tablet's dictionary, or go online to Wikipedia (or a more general search through Google) to read more about a word, name, or phrase. The same toolbar allows you to add a note to the beginning or end of a passage in a document, or to bookmark that page.

✔ A press-and-hold on the cover of a book or periodical in the Library allows you to send that publication to your personal archive. (It's not deleted, but you can't see it in your listing of current reading material.) Or you can delete a file using the same menu.

✔ When you're typing, press and hold a letter on the virtual keyboard to display accents, diacritical marks, and special characters.

✔ To open a file stored on a microSD/microSDHC memory card, go to the Library, tap the My Files icon, and press and hold a filename.

✔ A press-and-hold on the Home screen's wallpaper lets you choose a different background image: one of your own pictures, a supplied image, or an animated scene you can buy from the B&N app store.

✔ In the music player, a press-and-hold allows you to add a track to a playlist.

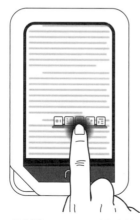

Figure 2-1: The press-and-hold is also known as a long press.

Swipe

I'm not advising you to steal a book. Swiping in this case means sliding your finger across the screen. See Figure 2-2. Think of it as using the left- or right-arrow keys on a computer keyboard. You can swipe to the left or to the right; you get a different effect depending on what type of file is open or where you are in the operating system.

Here are some examples of a swipe in use:

- ✔ In the Daily Shelf or your Library, swipe to move through a collection of items (such as a row of book covers).

- ✔ On the status bar, swiping to the left brings your NOOK Tablet back to the previous activity.

- ✔ When reading, swiping to the left will flip the page forward. Swiping from left to right takes you back a page.

Figure 2-2: Swipe to move side to side.

Scroll

A *scroll* is a vertical form of swipe; you move your finger up or down on the screen to go through a list. Think of it as using the up- or down-arrow keys on a computer keyboard.

For example:

- ✔ Scroll up or down through a list of menu options.
- ✔ Move down or go back up a set of thumbnail images of books, book pages, bookmarks, photos, or music tracks.
- ✔ Go through a magazine piece in Article view, zipping through the text without illustrations or photos.

Drag

When you drag on a touchscreen, you are — in an electronically metaphoric way — touching an object and pulling it to another location. Touch an object and keep your finger on it as you drag it where you want it to go; when the object is where you want it, lift your finger from the screen to leave the object in its new location.

Drag to these ends:

- ✔ Drag to check out additional web search results.
- ✔ Drag a piece of reading material from the Home screen to the Daily Shelf.
- ✔ Drag a slider left or right (or up or down) to adjust things like volume.
- ✔ Zip through the pages of a book by dragging the location slider right or left.
- ✔ Select a phrase by dragging a vertical bar (at either end of a word) until a pair of bars are around it.

✔ Drag crop marks to frame the part you want to keep of an image.

✔ Drag the virtual green ∩ symbol on the screen (not the physical one on the frame below) to the right to unlock the tablet and display the status bar.

Lift

You lift your finger from the screen when you're done making certain gestures such as dragging or pressing and holding. I tell you this just as a precautionary measure so that you don't feel you have to walk around for the rest of the week with your finger pressed tightly to the touchscreen.

Pinch

Ouch! A pinch is where you touch the two fingers on the touchscreen and bring two of them toward each other (or away from each other — aka a *pinch out*). Most people use their thumb and pointer finger. Pinch your fingers toward each other to shrink an image — a book cover or a photo, for example. Spread your fingers apart to zoom in on or enlarge an image on the screen. See Figure 2-3.

Figure 2-3: Pinch to zoom in or out on text or an image.

Press

The NOOK Tablet has four physical buttons: switches that you actually press. You don't tap, swipe, pinch, or anything else — just press.

- ✔ The first is the power button, at the top of the left side.

- ✔ Across the tablet, at the top of the right side, are pair of + and – volume control buttons.

- ✔ The ∩ button sits at the bottom of the screen as you hold it in portrait mode.

Seeing the Parts of the Whole

Aristotle, who to the best of my knowledge did not own a NOOK Tablet, is credited with saying, "The whole is greater than the sum of its parts." He said it in ancient Greece and in ancient Greek, but he could well have been considering the beauty of a modern electronic device.

Here's what I mean by that: The whole of the NOOK Tablet is made up of hundreds of different screens and uncounted features. The options screen for the web browser is completely different from the one for the music player, yet they share the same brain and screen and memory. In this section, we go through the main parts. See Figure 2-4.

Home screen

The Home screen is the default NOOK Tablet display (like the desktop on a personal computer). See Figure 2-5. The Home screen has two main areas:

- ✔ A desktop you can change, customize, and update.

- ✔ The Daily Shelf, which spreads across the bottom of the screen.

Reading now   Daily Shelf

Home screen
(NOOK) button   Status bar

Figure 2-4: The essential elements of the NOOK Tablet screen.

Panel indicators

Active panel

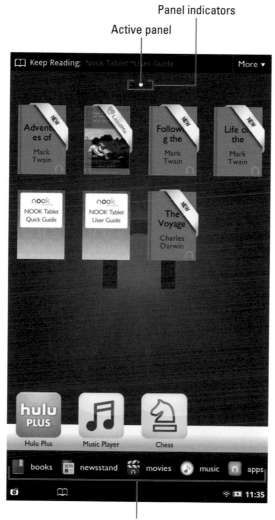

Media shortcuts

Figure 2-5: The NOOK Tablet's Home screen includes the desktop and the Daily Shelf.

The desktop of the Home screen and the Daily Shelf scroll independently of each other. Now I did just say that there were two main areas, and I'm not about to contradict myself in my own book. But there are a couple of less-than-main but still important sections of the Home screen:

> ✔ The Keep Reading menu, which is a small ribbon at the very top.
>
> ✔ Media shortcuts at the bottom.

I explain all four parts, plus more, in the following sections.

You can get back to the Home screen from anywhere by pressing the ∩ button on the front of the device.

Home screen desktop

The Home screen is subdivided into three panels you can use in most any way you want; only one of the three is active at a time, but the other two are waiting in the wings. You can drag and drop a book, magazine, newspaper, or document to any one of the panels if you want it immediately available for tapping.

Which of the panels are you looking at? Check the easily overlooked panel indicators at the top of the screen; they're pointed out in Figure 2-5. You'll see three small circles. The solid white circle shows which panel is active; the other two panels, available but not active, are shown as an open circle. To move from one panel to another, swipe your finger left or right across the screen.

Opening an item on the Daily Shelf or Home screen

Opening a book, magazine, newspaper, or app on the Home screen or Daily Shelf requires that you do one of these:

> ✔ Tap the icon for the item.
>
> ✔ Press and hold the icon for an item to display a menu. Then select Read. (Other choices, which may vary depending on the type of media or app, include View Details, Recommend, LendMe, and Remove from Home.)

Organizing your Home screen

The desk in my office is a pretty scary place, with piles of paper from each of the half dozen or so projects I'm usually working on at the same time. Don't let this happen to your Home screen. Organize and rearrange items.

Here's how to remove an item from the Home screen:

1. **Press and hold the item.**

   A menu appears.

2. **Tap Remove From Home.**

   The item is no longer shown on the Home screen, although you can get it if you burrow down into the stacks of your NOOK Tablet Library.

But wait, there's more. How about *rearranging* and *neatening* your Home screen? You can ask the tablet to do these house-keeping tasks:

- ✔ **Stack.** You can make your own pile of books, one on top of another. Just drag covers or icons on top of each other... up to a point: You can't completely hide any cover.

- ✔ **Grid.** If you want the tablet to automatically arrange all the covers in a neat grid, just double-tap any open area of the Home screen.

If you've got books stacked atop each other or haphazardly scattered around, you can also clean up an individual panel of the Home screen. See Figure 2-6. Here's how it appears onscreen:

1. **Press and hold a part of the wallpaper in the panel you want to clean up.**

   A menu appears.

2. **Tap Clean Up This Panel.**

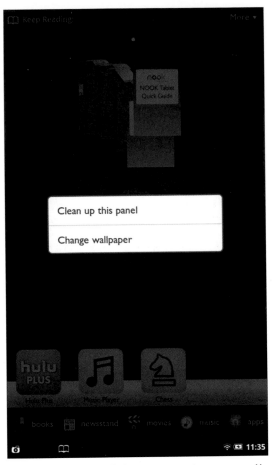

Figure 2-6: You can ask the system to clean up your Home screen. It won't ask for an allowance in return.

The Keep Reading (and More) Ribbon

Regardless of which panel of the Home screen you're consulting, you can access the Keep Reading ribbon at the top, as well as the More menu.

The Keep Reading ribbon lists whatever you were most recently reading. When you first start using your NOOK Tablet (or after you've done a major housecleaning project), there won't be any books or periodicals to *keep reading*, because you can't keep on keeping on with something you haven't yet begun. The ribbon will somewhat cryptically indicate: Keep Reading: None.

When you go to the Home screen, you'll see the title of your most recent piece of reading right there next to Keep Reading. And then, on the right side of the Keep Reading ribbon, you'll see the very promising More button.

To open the menu, tap the little down arrow next to More, which is in Figure 2-5. Here's what you'll see:

- ✔ **Books.** Titles and authors of the three books you most recently opened.

- ✔ **Periodicals.** Titles and publication dates of the three most recent periodicals you read.

- ✔ **Files.** Titles and types of the three files you most recently opened in the My Files folder.

- ✔ **Netflix.** Three recommendations from Netflix streaming video service, along with a link to log in to that service. (If you are already logged in, the menu shows your personal Netflix queue — movies you want to see — and three recommendations from it.)

If you haven't opened any books, newspapers, periodicals, personal files, documents, or Netflix movies, those categories won't appear on the menu.

The Daily Shelf

Give us this day our Daily Shelf, a row of books, magazines, newspapers, and applications that runs along the bottom of the Home screen. These are items that you have recently opened, bought, downloaded, borrowed, or otherwise received. You can manually move an item from your Library to the Daily Shelf. The latter holds only one issue of a magazine or newspaper; clicking *The New York Times* or *Sweet Potato Monthly* will open the most recent issue.

Leaving aside those that you have manually (digitally, actually, when you use your digits) moved there, the following brings an item into the leftmost place of honor on the Daily Shelf:

- ✔ Buying a book, magazine, newspaper, or app. Also, automatically receiving a new issue of a magazine or newspaper for which you have a subscription.

- ✔ Downloading a free book or app.

- ✔ Lending or borrowing a book. Getting a LendMe offer.

- ✔ Getting a recommendation from a friend.

- ✔ Opening an app that came with the tablet or one you bought from the NOOK Store.

New publications or apps are marked with a little flag. The Daily Shelf automatically puts the newest items on the left; that doesn't mean you have to keep the items in that order. To rearrange covers, place your finger on an item and drag it up about an inch and then left or right and down to a new position. This is a lot of fun — you'll feel very much like Moses parting the Red Sea: As you bring the item down, the books and magazines below it will move to make room. Just lift your finger and the book will go to its new home. Refer again to Figure 2-5.

Applications, or *apps,* are programs you can load onto your tablet to do certain things (play games, get directions, and so on). Read more about apps in Chapter 4.

When you remove an item from the Daily Shelf (or if it is automatically taken away because you have reached the limit of 50), it remains in your Library. Think of it like this: When something goes away from the Daily Shelf, it is returned to its regular place on the back shelves until you ask for it once more.

Media shortcuts

I know, I know: I said there were four main areas. This one is a fifth, but it's not a main one, and it's actually part of the Daily Shelf, and only sometimes. Media shortcuts are quick access to different types of media you recently accessed (as well as some brazenly commercial recommendations of similar items you just might want to buy from the NOOK store).

Tap any one of the icons if you want to see what your NOOK Tablet has in mind for you:

- Books
- Newsstand (magazines and newspapers)
- Video
- Music
- Apps

If you'd rather not have these on your Home screen, follow these steps:

1. **Touch the ⌒ button.**

   The quick nav bar comes up.

2. **Tap the Settings icon.**

3. **Tap the Home settings button.**

4. **Tap in the Media Shortcuts check box.**

Removing an item from the Daily Shelf

You don't have to wait for an item to be bumped from the Daily Shelf because of lack of room. If you want to get rid of a book shown there, you can remove it manually.

1. **Press and hold the item.**

   A menu appears.

2. **Tap Remove From Home.**

   That's it. The cover is removed from the Daily Shelf (and the Home screen, if it's also there). The item stays in your Library.

Going from the Daily Shelf to the Home screen, or vice versa

You can drag items from the Daily Shelf onto the Home screen. Items placed on a panel of the Home screen are always there to be seen (until you remove them), even if you pan left or right through the Daily Shelf. Here's how: Press and hold an icon in the Daily Shelf and keep your finger on it as you drag into an open area of the Home screen. When you lift your finger, the icon stays where you put it, and the Daily Shelf neatens itself up. To return an item from the Home screen to the Daily Shelf, press and hold the item and drag it back down to the bottom.

Wallpaper

The 16-million-color high-resolution display that sits behind the Home screen is a terrible thing to waste. You can select from patterns and pictures that come with the tablet, but why not post one of your own photos as the wallpaper?

You can change the wallpaper from the Home screen or by going to the Settings screen.

1. **On the Home screen, press and hold the existing wallpaper.**

   A menu appears.

2. **Tap Change Wallpaper.**

   Another dialog box offers two choices.

3. **Tap Wallpaper Gallery or Photo Gallery.**

   Wallpaper is already on the NOOK Tablet. The photo gallery has images that come from one of these sources:

   • An image you have directly downloaded to your NOOK Tablet from a website or grabbed as a screen capture. (I explain how to do this in Chapter 5.)

   • An image you transferred to the NOOK Tablet from a personal computer. (The image could, in turn, come from your digital camera or from a download from the Internet.) I use as my wallpaper a photo I took of a field of sunflowers near Seville, Spain; I processed it on my desktop computer to make it appear in the style of painter Georges Seurat. See Figure 2-7.

Figure 2-7: My wallpaper is a photo I took in Spain.

After you choose between Wallpaper Gallery or Photo Gallery, a new screen allows you to scroll through images until you find one you want to use. If you choose an image from the photo gallery, you can crop it to fit best. You need a vertical photo or drawing to fill the Home screen. (Images in the wallpaper gallery are already fitted for prime time.)

If you decide you don't want to change the wallpaper, tap anywhere outside the dialog box to close the menu. Or click the Cancel button in the gallery menu.

4. Tap the Set Wallpaper button.

Checking Your Status Bar

The status bar is on the bottom of the touchscreen and shows up when you need it; in general, it stays out of the way when you want to do something else (like read a book, watch a video, or browse the Internet). See Figure 2-8. When describing the status bar, I divide up the information by left, center, and right side.

Figure 2-8: The status bar looks different depending on what you're doing.

Left

No, your other left.

- At the left side of the bar you may see a green ∩ symbol, which tells you new software updates have been installed. All by themselves.

- An envelope with an @ is a pronouncement that "You've got mail."

- Downward-pointing arrows tell you that new books, periodicals, or apps are in the process of *downloading* (being put on your tablet).

- An open book stands ready to return you to the book you were most recently reading.

- A red circle with a number informs you of notifications your tablet has received for LendMe, recommendations, software updates, or other system information.

- If you're listening to Pandora, a stylized P tells you music is in the air. (And unless you have the volume turned off, you already know that.)

- When the music player is doing its thing, an icon or red musical notes appears; tap it to return to the controls for that program.

- A pair of heads appears when the NOOK Friends app has gotten an update; new contacts or other social items may have arrived.

- Depending on what you've most recently been doing, you may see a left-pointing arrow that can take you to a previous activity. (If not, there hasn't been an activity the NOOK considers worth revisiting.)

Right

And then over there on the right, here's what you've got:

- The stack of little curves is your wireless connection indicator. The higher the stack, the stronger the signal. No curves, no connection. Two or three curves are a good connection.

- If the battery is full, so too is the actual battery in the tablet. If it is half-full, that's half as good. If the battery is nearly empty, find an electrical outlet and attach the charger.

- The clock is set like usual, but if you visit the Time Settings screen you can change it to a 24-hour clock.

  The clock has to display the correct time. The official time on your NOOK Tablet is used in regards to updates, downloads, and synchronized bookmarks.

- A small speaker with a slash through it means you've muted the sound. You can unmute or adjust the volume of the audio in the Quick Settings window or in the full Settings menu.

Another *as-you-need-it* menu is available from the status bar. Tap the right corner of the bar near the battery status indicator to open the Quick Settings dialog box. To close the Quick Settings dialog box, tap anywhere outside the box. That dialog box is even quicker than the quick nav bar. See Figure 2-9.

Figure 2-9: The Quick Settings dialog box usually offers a logical guess at immediate needs.

The Quick Settings dialog box has these settings:

✓ **Battery.** Right off the bat is an entry that's not really a setting. Its bar graph and percentage tell you the status of the rechargeable battery. A full bar and 100% are roughly twice as good as a half bar and 50%. The display also tells you if the NOOK Tablet is currently (get it?) being charged.

✔ **WiFi Toggle Switch.** Drag the WiFi toggle to On to turn on the wireless radio; Off shuts its down, which helps save battery power. When your NOOK Tablet is connected to a network, you will see the name of the network in use.

✔ **Mute.** Tap the check box to mute or unmute beeps or squawks from the system meant as notification.

✔ **Auto-Rotate Screen.** When you go online or read certain documents, the NOOK Tablet automatically switches orientation when you rotate it. The standard orientation for the NOOK Tablet is what computer folk call *portrait mode* (as in a painting of a human being in an art gallery). If you rotate the tablet, it switches to landscape mode. That brings you to the Auto-Rotate Screen check box: Tap it to turn the feature on or off.

✔ **Brightness.** Tap to open a dialog box that has a slider, so you can make the screen brighter or dimmer. A dimmed screen may be easier on your eyes and save a bit of battery power, allowing you to read longer between recharges. After moving the slider, tap OK to put your preference into effect.

In the middle: Quick nav bar

There when you need it (but absent when you don't), the quick nav bar is the superhighway to some important functions. To display the bar, touch the ∩ button on the lower front frame of the tablet. You can get to most of what the quick nav bar has in other ways, but here they're quicker (imagine!) to navigate to. See Figure 2-10. Once the bar appears, tap one of these choices:

✔ Home

✔ Library

✔ Shop

✔ Search

✔ Apps

✔ Web

✔ Settings

Figure 2-10: You can jump from the quick nav bar to any of the tablet's main functions.

Home

If, perchance, you should happen to be away from home — on any other page of the NOOK Tablet or out on the Internet — tap this virtual button to go back to the main screen, which holds the Daily Shelf. The Home screen also has any other books, publications, or apps you copied onto it.

Library

Tapping here opens the portal to all your tablet's literary content. Buttons at the top take you to shelves. For each, you can choose an organizational scheme. Four of the six sections here (Books, Magazines, Newspaper, and My Stuff) let you choose how the titles are displayed. That organization becomes more important as you acquire more to read. See Figure 2-11.

The button that looks like a stack of books is the icon for the Library itself. Tap that button and choose among these options:

- A three-by-three grid of book covers.
- Shelves that separate books and other documents by the date you last read them.
- A detailed list of documents, with a small cover and a summary of the contents.
- A list of even smaller documents, along with the title and author's name.

Figure 2-11: The Library neatly organizes books, magazines, apps, and other content.

These categories are in the Library:

Books. All the documents that are classified as books. Generally, this means EPUB and some PDF files. If you have your own files or imported public-domain books, they may show up here as books or they may appear in My Files.

✓ **Magazines.** The covers of the most recent editions of magazines you subscribe to, or individual issues you bought.

✓ **Newspapers.** The front pages of the most recent editions of newspapers, whether you bought just a single edition or you're subscribed.

✓ **Apps.** You can add new features by installing *apps* (short for *applications,* which are small software programs). I discuss apps in detail in Chapter 4.

✓ **Kids.** Because even if they can't read, there are books out there for them. See Chapter 3 for more.

✓ **My Stuff.** As the great George Carlin more or less said, your NOOK Tablet is just a place to hold your stuff. My Stuff holds the following:

- **My Shelves.** No assembly required. Tap the virtual onscreen keyboard to label shelves. I added a Faves shelf. Another shelf, titled Lectures, holds presentation notes that I carry on the device.

- **My Files.** Here is any content that you've side-loaded onto your tablet from a laptop or personal computer. You will see icons for the folders, very much like you would see on a personal computer; see Figure 2-12. Tap one of the folders to open it. I explore side-loading in Chapter 3.

- **LendMe.** Here you can see the books in your collection that you can loan to others, any books you've borrowed, and any offers made or received for lending or borrowing. I discuss the lending program in Chapter 3.

- **Archived.** Here are books or other files you have archived. Your files are still on the tablet and available but they're no longer among current titles.

Figure 2-12: My Stuff has documents, downloads, photos, and other material you have added to your tablet.

Shop

Click here to move to the Barnes & Noble NOOK store. (If you haven't enabled the WiFi system, you end up at the screen where you can turn it on. And, of course, you have to be within range of a WiFi network that will allow you to connect.)

Just about every time you visit the site, you'll see a different display; some of the recommendations are based on your previous purchases and others are ads for books being promoted by the store. I discuss the shopping experience in Chapter 4.

If you shop at another store, not owned and operated by B&N, you'll have to get to that site by using the web browser.

Search

The tab gets you into the NOOK Tablet's search screen, where you can hunt for any file or app on your device, as well as on the Barnes & Noble NOOK store or the web. Use the onscreen virtual keyboard to enter some of the name you're looking for; the screen will almost immediately begin listing possibilities. The more letters you enter, the narrower the list becomes. You can tap any item in the list to go to it, and you can also tap Search Web or Search Wikipedia to go out on the Internet (with an active WiFi connection) to find out more.

Apps

Here's where the NOOK Tablet shows that it's more than a mere eBook reader. Apps add new features to your device. Tapping here gives you access to extras supplied with the NOOK Tablet (including Contacts, Email, NOOK Friends, Hulu Plus, Pandora, and games), as well as apps you may buy from the NOOK store.

I discuss the supplied apps and the B&N NOOK Store in detail in Chapter 4.

Web

Tap here to open the NOOK Tablet Web Browser and move onto the Internet, through an enabled WiFi connection. Read more in Chapter 5.

If the Web button is grayed out (not all bright and colorful) and it shows "Disabled," the browser can't respond. The solution: Reactivate it. To do that, go to Settings and choose the browser control panel; from there, reactivate the browser.

Settings

From here you can navigate, quickly, to the myriad settings panels for everything from the screen brightness, audio volume, WiFi connection nitty-gritty, and much more. I discuss configuring your NOOK Tablet in the following section.

Configuring Your NOOK Tablet

The basic control panel is the Settings tool, which lets you customize your NOOK Tablet's wireless, screen, sound, security, keyboard, and other features.

Take these steps to display the Settings menu:

1. **Tap the ∩ button to open the quick nav bar.**

2. **In the quick nav bar, tap the Settings icon.**

 From any customization section, you can return to the main settings screen by tapping the back arrow at the top-left corner of a page. From the Settings panel, press the ∩ button to return to the Home screen or one of the other options including your Library, the web, or apps.

The main settings page is divided into two parts: Device Settings and App Settings. See Figure 2-13.

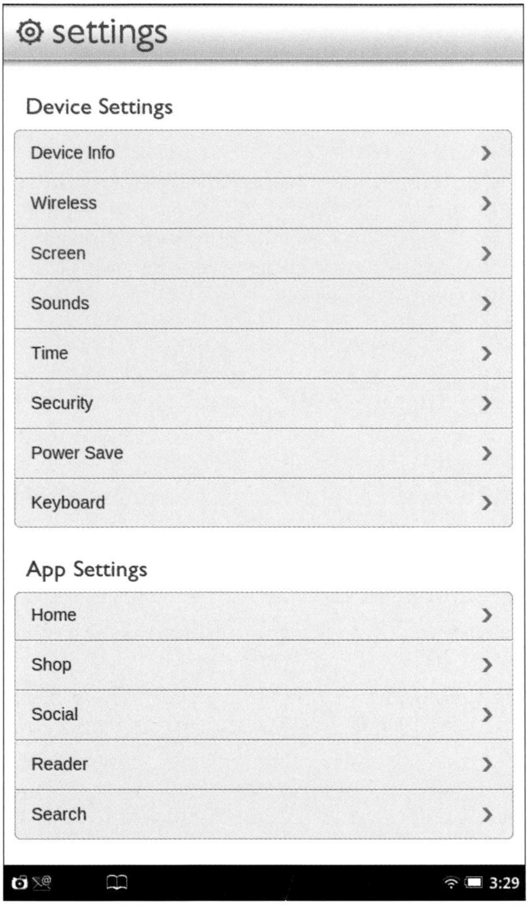

⚙ settings

Device Settings

Device Info	>
Wireless	>
Screen	>
Sounds	>
Time	>
Security	>
Power Save	>
Keyboard	>

App Settings

Home	>
Shop	>
Social	>
Reader	>
Search	>

🗖 🗙 📖 📶 ▯ 3:29

Figure 2-13: The main portal to your tablet's personality is the Device Settings menu.

Device Settings

Device settings help you customize some of the essential hardware features, including the battery.

Device Info

The data displayed here, shown in Figure 2-14, includes the following:

✔ **Battery.** A precise measurement of the percentage of charge remaining in the internal battery. If the device is charging, you'll see that (along with a bright orange on the USB cable near the port where it connects to the NOOK Tablet). Otherwise, you can see the battery is being used.

✔ **B&N Content Storage Available.** The total amount of available flash memory in the device that is available to hold items purchased from Barnes & Noble. It is expressed as an absolute number (11.60GB of 11.87GB, for example) as well as a percentage (98%) in this example. When you delete a book or file, the memory space devoted to it is made available for other uses.

✔ **Other Storage Available.** About 1GB of the built-in *(internal)* memory is available for documents, pictures, music, video, and other files. Again, you'll see an absolute number and a percentage.

✔ **SD Card.** If you've installed a microSD or microSDHC card in the available slot, its capacity and available storage space are listed here. This storage space is yours, yours, yours. If you install a 32GB card (the maximum), you can use as much of it as you want for whatever you want.

✔ **About Your NOOK.** Tap the right-facing arrow to see the name of the owner and the Barnes & Noble account title, as well as hardware specifics, including the model number, serial number, WiFi MAC address, and the operating system version number.

✔ **Erase & Deregister Device.** Stop. Wait. Don't tap this option unless you have a *real* good reason to do so. Any personal files you have moved to the NOOK Tablet will be deleted from the device. The command also removes all books (no matter their source), and removes the details that your device uses to identify itself to the Barnes & Noble website. However, any titles you bought from Barnes & Noble are linked to your account, and if you re-register your NOOK Tablet to that account, the previously deleted books go back onto your NOOK Tablet.

You may want to use Erase & Deregister in two situations:

- Your device gets corrupted or unresponsive and customer support suggests you use it.

- You sell or give your NOOK Tablet to someone else but want to keep your associated B&N account.

✔ **Legal.** If you're really, really bored and are completely out of anything else to read, you might want to peruse the legal notices and credits listed here. Or perhaps you need something to help you fall asleep. Great literature is found elsewhere.

Wireless

This page has a virtual switch for the WiFi circuitry; tap it to turn on the radio; tap it again to turn it off. When the WiFi switch is on, you can see all the wireless networks the NOOK Tablet can find in its neighborhood. I discuss wireless communication in detail in Chapter 5.

Screen

Three important touchscreen controls are here:

✔ **Auto-rotate screen.** Tell the NOOK Tablet to switch to landscape if you've rotated the reader to horizontal and then back to portrait when you rotate it to an upright position. This feature generally works only in the web browser, magazines, and the photo gallery. You can turn this feature on or off by checking the Orientation check box. When unchecked, the NOOK Tablet stays in portrait mode at all times.

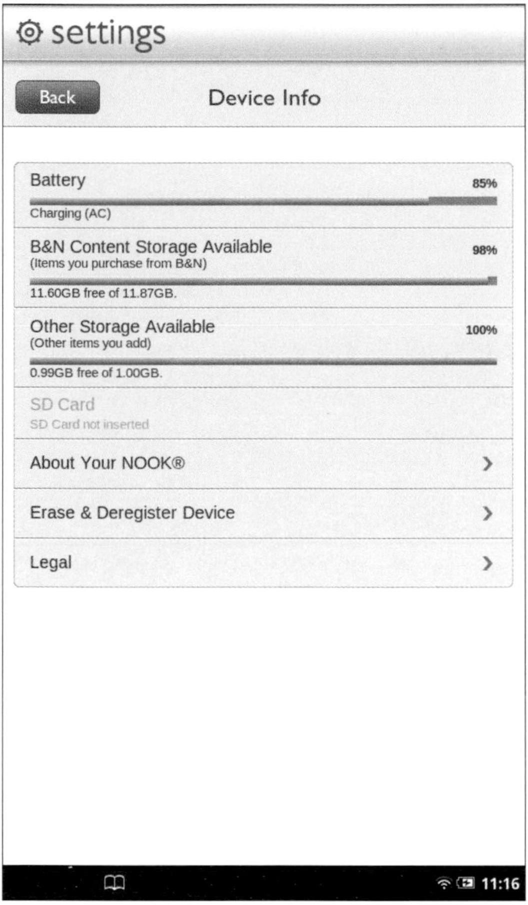

⚙ settings

| Back | Device Info |

Battery 85%
Charging (AC)

B&N Content Storage Available 98%
(Items you purchase from B&N)

11.60GB free of 11.87GB.

Other Storage Available 100%
(Other items you add)

0.99GB free of 1.00GB.

SD Card
SD Card not inserted

About Your NOOK® >

Erase & Deregister Device >

Legal >

📖 🛜 🔋 11:16

Figure 2-14: Device Info tells you about battery status and available storage space.

📑 **Brightness.** This, of course, has nothing to do with the IQ of your tablet, but rather with the intensity of the backlighting. Drag the slider from dim to bright or back. A bright light might help in a dark room, but you may find it causes eyestrain; a dimmer backlight may improve readability outdoors. In any case, a lower level of brightness will use less battery power. Choose the lighting level that works best for you and adjust it as needed when conditions change.

✓ **Screen timeout.** To save battery power, the NOOK Tablet
will turn off its screen after you haven't done anything
with it; the standard setting is 2 minutes. You can change
it to 5 minutes, 15 minutes, or 1 hour. See Figure 2-15.
You'll have a few seconds' advance notice before the
tablet goes to sleep: The screen dims slightly. When the
screen shuts off, you can turn it back on again by pressing the Home button and swiping the wake-up bar from
left to right.

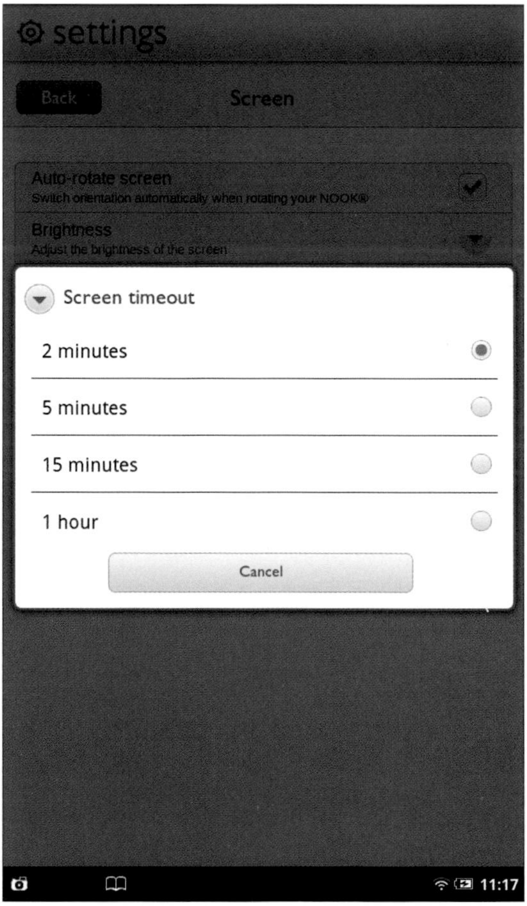

Figure 2-15: Adjusting Screen Timeout to match your use patterns can help save battery power.

Sounds

If only I could have installed this control on my children as they grew up; it would have added years to my life. Under Sounds, you can mute or unmute the system notification beeps that the tablet makes, as well as the speaker volume for music and video. Read Chapter 4 for more on sound.

These are the controls:

🖝 **Mute.** Tap here to turn on or off system notification sounds and keyboard clicks. When the check box is checked, these sounds are muted; when the box is empty, they're on. If you're reading in a library (can you imagine?), you might want to shush your NOOK Tablet before Marian the Librarian does it for you.

🖝 **Media.** Press the slider to control the volume for music and videos. You'll hear a sound to indicate the loudness you've chosen. Tap OK to make the setting.

🖝 **Notification.** Press the slider to control the volume for system notifications (such as low battery level). A sample sound indicates the loudness you have chosen. Tap OK to make the setting.

Control the speaker volume with the + and – volume buttons on the right edge of the device. The volume controls on the Sounds settings page also control volume. If you turn down the volume on the Settings page, you can turn up the noise with the physical buttons (or the other way around).

Time

Your clock in the lower-right corner is used for the alarm and calendar apps. And it is also part of the synchronization process when you get new reading material from Barnes & Noble. That's why you have to make sure it's set correctly; you don't want to accidentally get rid of books. You can set the clock format and time zone.

🖝 **Use 24-hour format.** Tap in the box to turn on a 24-hour clock; see you at 17:30 for cocktails in the office lounge.

🖝 **Select time zone.** As delivered, the device shows only time zones in the United States; to see a list of all time zones around the world, tap the Show All World Time Zones check box. It's a pretty complete list, including Newfoundland time, which sits half an hour between Greenland and Atlantic time, and even Kathmandu, which operates at Greenwich Mean Time +5:45. See Figure 2-16.

⚙ settings

| Back | Time Zone |

| Midway Island |
| GMT-11:00 |

| Hawaii |
| GMT-10:00 |

| Alaska |
| GMT-9:00 |

| Pacific Time |
| GMT-8:00 |

| Tijuana |
| GMT-8:00 |

| Arizona |
| GMT-7:00 |

| Chihuahua |
| GMT-7:00 |

| Mountain Time |
| GMT-7:00 |

| Central America |
| GMT-6:00 |

| Central Time |
| GMT-6:00 |

| Mexico City |
| GMT-6:00 |

| Saskatchewan |
| GMT-6:00 |

| Bogota |
| GMT-5:00 |

✅ Show all world time zones

2:56

Figure 2-16: Keep your NOOK Tablet on time by selecting the local time zone.

Security

Life used to be so much simpler (though not necessarily better) when all we had to worry about was losing a wallet that held walking-around money and a driver's license. Now we carry smartphones, tablets, and laptops that hold our entire financial, medical, and personal details. That's why I believe deeply in passwords that look like expletives: 6h!x%r^&#.

> ✔ **Device Lock Passcode.** Here you can require that any user enter a four-digit password to turn on the NOOK Tablet or wake it from sleep. Use this feature if you worry that unauthorized people may try to use your reader: strangers or your children, for example.

> ✔ **Restrictions.** You can add a secondary password that locks away access to the web browser and/or social media like Facebook and Twitter and also prevents the sharing of recommendations. You might want to do this to keep the kids away from unsupervised surfing or to protect personal information from unauthorized eyes.

Want a good reason to add a device lock passcode? Your Barnes & Noble account has your credit card number stored away. That means someone else could, in theory, buy something at B&N without your permission.

Power Save

Although you can adjust things like screen brightness, screen timeout, and other features, tapping the Power Save check box will turn on a preset scheme that's supposed to help the battery last.

Keyboard

Here's where you can customize the virtual onscreen keyboard. To configure the keyboard, tap Keyboard from the Settings screen. The available options are listed here:

> ✔ **Keyboard Sounds.** Turn on or off a clicking sound when you tap the keys. The click is pretty quiet, but it does confirm that your taps have registered.

> ✔ **Auto-Capitalization.** The system will capitalize names and initial words in recommendations and reviews.

✔ **Quick Fixes.** The computer can correct some typing errors. Tap the check box by any option you want to change. A checkmark means the option is turned on; the absence of a checkmark shows it's disabled.

App Settings

The group of settings here help you customize some of the personality of the operating system that runs on your NOOK Tablet as well as some of the supplied apps.

General Home Settings

There's no place like it. See Figure 2-17.

✔ **Set Wallpaper.** This is one way you can choose a predesigned background for your Home screen, or select an image you've loaded into the photo gallery of the NOOK Tablet from a laptop or personal computer. Tap the down arrow to see a menu with two tabs: Wallpapers and Photo Gallery (images you put on the tablet). If you've bought *live wallpapers,* which dance and fly and are otherwise animated, there will be a third collection from which you can choose.

✔ **Clear Keep Reading List.** You'll be asked to confirm your decision.

✔ **Clear Daily Shelf.** You're sure?

✔ **Media Shortcuts.** If you don't want to see that extra level of shortcut icons that appear below the Daily Shelf (including both recently accessed items for books, music, video, and the like as well as recommendations for similar items you might like to purchase), clear the check box here.

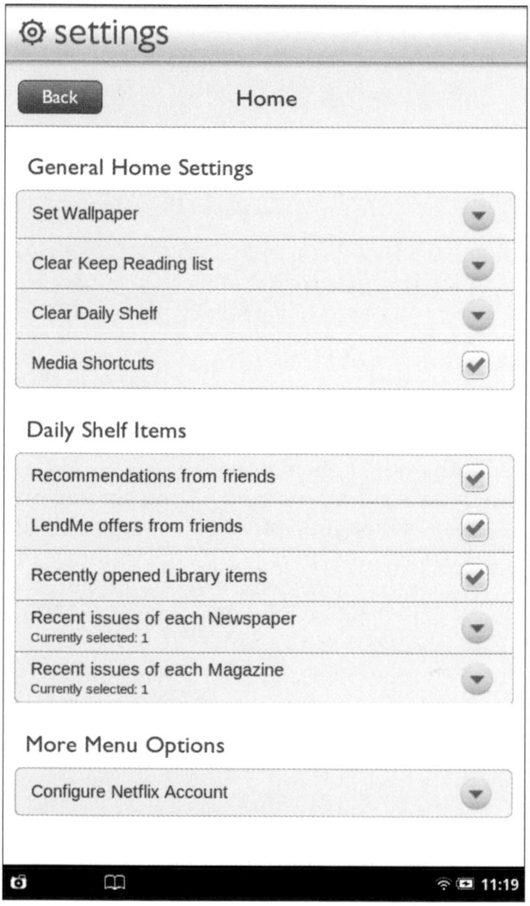

⚙ settings

Back	Home

General Home Settings

Set Wallpaper ▾

Clear Keep Reading list ▾

Clear Daily Shelf ▾

Media Shortcuts ☑

Daily Shelf Items

Recommendations from friends ☑

LendMe offers from friends ☑

Recently opened Library items ☑

Recent issues of each Newspaper
Currently selected: 1 ▾

Recent issues of each Magazine
Currently selected: 1 ▾

More Menu Options

Configure Netflix Account ▾

📷 📖 📶 🔋 11:19

Figure 2-17: The general Home Settings allow you to personalize the components of the desktop and Daily Shelf.

Daily Shelf Items

Here you can turn on or off, or for some options, make selections that affect the way the Daily Shelf appears. The changes you make here don't block any items, but just move them a bit deeper so you don't have to see them except when you want to.

- **Recommendations from Friends.** Clear the check box to avoid seeing them on the Daily Shelf.

- **LendMe Offers From Friends.** Yes or no.

✓ **Recently Opened Library items.** Again, your choice.

✓ **Recent Issues of Each Newspaper.** Press the down arrow to select the number of issues you want to be noted: 1, 2, 3, or all.

✓ **Recent Issues of Each Magazine.** Just like for newspapers, except for magazines.

More Menu Options

Well, the screen uses the plural, but when the NOOK Tablet came out there was just a single option:

✓ **Configure Netflix Account.** Tapping the down arrow connects you to a login screen for a *pre-existing account* with Netflix. What you're doing here is linking your Barnes & Noble account to Netflix so you can get recommendations and place orders. I discuss Netflix and other supplied apps in Chapter 5.

Shop

For some, their home away from home. You know who you are.

✓ **Require Password for Purchases.** If you tap this check box, you (or anyone else in possession of your NOOK Tablet) will have to enter a password before buying something from the Barnes & Noble website. Yes, I know you might have already required a Device Lock.

✓ **Manage Credit Card.** To have a working account with Barnes & Noble, you must register a credit card with the company. Tapping Manage Credit Card allows you to view your current default card (all but the last four digits are blanked out). Tap the Change Default Credit Card to do just that. You can register only one card to the account, but you can change it any time on this page. See Figure 2-18.

✓ **Add Gift Card.** This nice feature isn't yet found on many other online shopping sites: you can enter the codes for as many as three gift cards, eGift cards issued electronically, or online gift certificates. The combined value of the cards is credited to your account and any future Barnes & Noble purchases you make with your online account will first be deducted from this total.

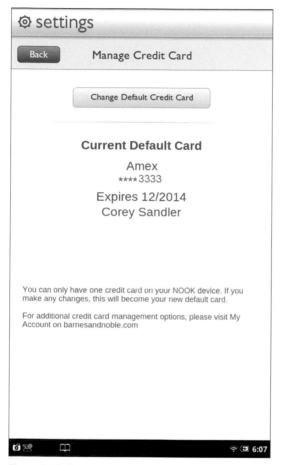

⚙ settings

| Back | Manage Credit Card |

Change Default Credit Card

Current Default Card

Amex
****3333

Expires 12/2014
Corey Sandler

You can only have one credit card on your NOOK device. If you
make any changes, this will become your new default card.

For additional credit card management options, please visit My
Account on barnesandnoble.com

🎦 6:07

Figure 2-18: You can manage the credit card associated with your B&N account.

✔ **Clear Shop Recent Searches.** A bit awkwardly phrased, this control erases the history of all searches you have made on the B&N website; you can select this as a matter of privacy or just to clean your device of extraneous information.

Social

To some, the web is their oyster. Social networking on Facebook and exchanging life's minute details with Twitter fit seamlessly into the world of NOOK Friends. If that describes you, here are the missing links:

- *Manage Your Accounts.* You can link your Facebook, Twitter, or Google Mail accounts, which allows quick message exchange. It also lets you make or accept LendMe offers. Enter your login and password details for each service.

- *Add Facebook Friends as NOOK Friends.* If you've set up a Facebook page, and if you've been friended by those you know best (and some who know you least), add their connection information so they can share books, recommendations, and comments using the NOOK Friends network.

Reader

Reader is the app that lets the NOOK Tablet read eBooks. Most of Reader's functions are set (or you can adjust them on the pages of books and magazines). But on this setting page, you have one further option: Animate eBook Page Turns. This tiny bit of micromanaging is one that some readers really enjoy: A checkmark in this box (the default) makes pages slide smoothly across the screen as you turn the pages of an eBook.

Search

Now where in the world did I put that magazine, and how can I find the song I bought because of the profile of the artist I read there? You can adjust where a Search command will hunt. You can also clear recent searches so that they don't reappear as suggestions when you start a new hunt. Read more in Chapter 3.

In this section of Settings, you can choose **Searchable Items.** Tap the down arrow and indicate the system where you want to hunt:

- ✔ **Web.** Look on the Internet as well as in your browser history and bookmarks.

- ✔ **Apps.** Include the names of applications you've installed.

- ✔ **Music player.** Check the names of artists, albums, and tracks.

Although these two options are grayed out, your NOOK Tablet will *always* look in your Library of books, magazines, and newspapers, and will also *always* check out the B&N Shop.

Configuring security settings

If your Nook Tablet never leaves your bedside table, you might consider it safe from intrusion. That is, if you have no fears that your significant other, children, friends, family, or the cable television repair guy will ever touch it. And say you do take the device with you to work or when you travel; now you have to worry about loss or theft or unwanted intrusions.

I strongly suggest protecting access with a general password. What exactly are you guarding? All of your personal information, any files stored on the internal memory, any settings and configurations, your web browsing settings and login information, and the details you have recorded with the Barnes & Noble store. A password *doesn't* protect the contents of any microSD or microSDHC memory card you have installed in the device's expansion slot if someone were to remove that card and read it on another device. See Figure 2-19.

To tell your Nook Tablet to lock the screen after a certain number of minutes of inactivity and to require a four-digit passcode to unlock it, do this:

1. **Press the ∩ button to display the quick nav bar.**

2. **Tap Settings.**

3. **On the Settings screen, tap Security in the Device Settings panel.**

4. **Tap the Device Lock Passcode check box.**

5. **Type a four-digit password.**

6. **Enter the code again.**

⚙ settings

Enter passcode

1	2 ABC	3 DEF
4 GHI	5 JKL	6 MNO
7 PQRS	8 TUV	9 WXYZ
Cancel	0	⌫

📷　📖　　　　　　　🛜 ▣ 11:19

Figure 2-19: The key to unlocking a password is a four-digit number of your choice.

Choose a four-digit passcode you will remember, but not one as obvious as the last four digits of your phone number or your Social Security number. Instead, how about the last four digits (or the first four digits) of a phone number of a friend or a business not directly associated with you?

You can turn off the passcode:

1. **Press the ⋂ button to display the quick nav bar.**
2. **Tap Settings.**
3. **On the Settings screen, tap Security in the Device Settings panel.**
4. **Tap the Device Lock Passcode check box.**

   The checkmark is removed.

5. **Type the four-digit password you had been using.**

Chapter 3

Loading and Reading

1 suppose the teacher and writer Marshall McLuhan had it mostly right when he said, "The medium is the message." It's not that the content doesn't matter, but as technologies advance and change, the delivery system — the medium — becomes linked with the message it carries. Enough of the philosophical discourse. Forget for a moment about the technology: The NOOK Tablet is merely another way to read the printed word and absorb its content into our souls.

This chapter looks at the NOOK Tablet as an eReader for books, newspapers, magazines, and most other electronic documents. You discover how to locate, open, read, bookmark, and reshelve documents. Then I tell you how to stock the shelves with purchases from the Barnes & Noble bookstore and with free downloads from other sources, and how to move books, documents, and other files from your personal computer to your tablet.

Knowing Your PDF from Your EPUB

Before you start worrying about file format, here's the deal: If you purchase or download a book or other publication from the Barnes & Noble online store, it will work on your NOOK Tablet. And the same should apply to any major third-party online bookseller or free source (like Google Books).

Remember: I'm talking about books here. Your NOOK Tablet can also display word processing, spreadsheet, presentation, and other files. And I show you how to create your own EPUB and PDF files as well. But not in this chapter; that happens in Chapter 4.

Both EPUB and PDF file types come in two types: protected and unprotected. A *protected* book has digital rights management (DRM) restrictions. Basically, there's some limit on whether (or how often) you can make copies, lend, or transfer the title to another. Nearly every professional author and publisher supports the concept of DRM. Please don't attempt to pick a fight with me about this: Authors need to pay their mortgage and put food on the table, just like you.

EPUB

If you have a choice, go for EPUB so that you have the widest variety of customization and special features. If you can't get an EPUB, PDF may be acceptable to most readers. Here are some details:

EPUBs are free and open (meaning that anyone can produce and distribute a file using this standard). That doesn't mean you can release a document based on copyrighted material that belongs to someone else. An EPUB file is reflowable, meaning you can change font, font size, and other things.

PDF

These files can be created in either of two rather different forms. More advanced PDFs can include fonts and images, and will let you enlarge pages. However, some PDFs are scans (think of them as snapshots), like the one shown in Figure 3-1. They may look fine on your NOOK Tablet, or you may need to adjust the zoom and move around on each individual page to read the text. And these most primitive of eBooks don't allow you to change font or size and don't link to the web.

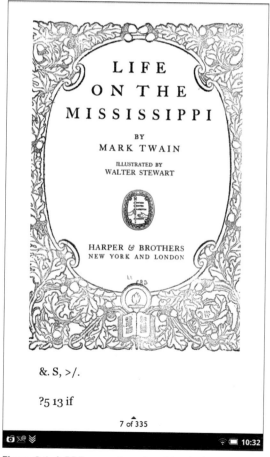

Figure 3-1: A PDF scan of a printed book gives you a set of pictures of pages rather than reflowable, searchable text.

Taking a Crack at Reading Tools

The pathway to the bells and whistles lies in the Reading Tools menu. Here is where you can move quickly through a book, search for something in particular, share your knowledge, or change the way the page looks. See Figure 3-2.

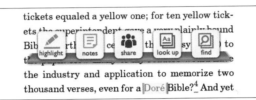

Figure 3-2: Reading tools let you highlight or make notes, look up words, and search the document.

To display the reading tools, tap near the center of the page.

Above these basic tools is a slider; it's a gray line with a blue dot somewhere along its path. The location of the dot shows where you are in the book. To move forward or backward quickly, touch and drag the slider right or left. If you're reading a book that someone has loaned you, a button at the right end of the slider lets you buy your own copy. And then, if the book publisher has included this feature, you may see a small blue flag all the way to the right end of the slider. Tap that flag to see special options related to that book; you may see recommendations for similar books or content that's included just with the eBook.

To quickly jump to a particular page, tap the Go to Page button (between the reading tools and the slider). A numeric keypad will appear and you can enter a specific page number; keep in mind that page numbering is relative. If you have changed the typeface or its size, the book will reflow and page numbers will change.

Content

Select this to open up a menu with three tabs, including — as advertised — Contents. Here are the purposes of the three tabs:

✔ **Contents.** A list of chapter titles, sometimes with subsections. The current chapter is highlighted by a gray bar. In most books you can jump immediately to a section by tapping the title or subsection name.

✔ **Notes & Highlights.** A list of passages that you've highlighted or written notes about in the current book. Again, you can jump to any of them by tapping the item.

✔ **Bookmarks.** A list of all bookmarks you've set in the current title. Jump to any of the pages by tapping its notation.

Find

Use the computer's power to find a particular word or phrase anywhere in the book.

1. **Tap Search.**

   A keyboard appears onscreen.

2. **Type a word or phrase you want to search for in the book.**

3. **Tap the Search button in the lower-right corner of the screen.**

Share

Got something you'd like to tell others about? This tool links to social networking sites like Twitter or to e-mail, and from there to your friends, family, and business associates. A sub-menu offers these choices:

✔ **Recommend.** Praise a book to friends and acquaintances by sending e-mail, posting a recommendation on your Facebook wall (or that of a friend who granted you that permission), or tweeting through your Twitter account.

✔ **Post Reading Status.** You can tell others how far you've gotten in the current book by posting a message on Facebook or Twitter. Why? I'm really not sure, but someone must be interested in such matters.

✔ **Rate and Review.** Send your comments and a 1–5 rating for display on BN.com, or post your review on Facebook or Twitter.

✔ **Like on Facebook.** Proclaim to the world (or at least those who read your Facebook news feed) that you really, really like this book.

Before you can use e-mail or social network services, you have to link your NOOK Tablet to your Facebook or Twitter accounts (see Figure 3-3) or add e-mail accounts to the Contacts application.

Figure 3-3: If you don't already have a Twitter account, you can sign up for one from the tablet.

Text

Gutenberg could never have imagined this. This menu, for reasons known only to the designers at B&N, has a different look and feel than most of the other options screens in the tablet. Never mind, though; it's pretty easy to use. See Figure 3-4, which shows the boxes.

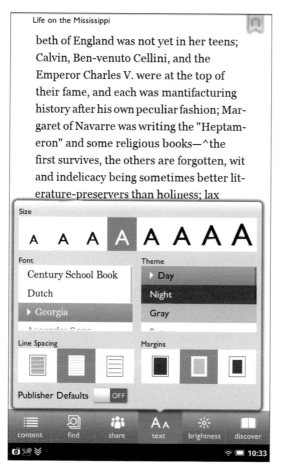

Figure 3-4: Text settings include size, font, line spacing, margins, text color, and background color.

Size

In most EPUB books, and in many PDFs, you can choose from eight type sizes. You just see eight A characters. Start out at the fifth or sixth largest for a good balance between readability and number of words that fit on the page. Feel free to experiment, though; touching any of the A's will instantly change the size of the type that still shows above the menu.

Font

The NOOK Tablet comes with six different type styles. (Some book publishers may limit the options, though.) The first three typefaces are *serif* style, like the face used in most newspapers and magazines; many of the characters have extra little straight or curved marks that many readers find to be easier to read. The last three styles are *sans serifs* fonts, which means "without serifs."

Theme

With an advanced eReader and a color LCD, you can choose the "paper" and the lighting:

- **Day.** This is your basic black text against white background.

- **Night.** You guessed this: white type against a black or gray background. This may be useful for reading at night or in other dark environments where you don't want to light up the room with your book.

- **Gray.** Black text on a light gray background. It isn't a bad occasional choice to rest your weary eyes.

- **Butter.** A slight variation on day, using dark brown text against a pale yellow page.

- **Mocha.** White text against a light brown backdrop.

- **Sepia.** Black text against a yellow-brown page.

Line Spacing

You can adjust the amount of space between lines of text: single spacing, 1.5-line spacing, and double spacing, shown from left to right onscreen.

Margins

Experiment here between narrow, medium, and wide margins for the text. The more white space there is around the text, the fewer words will fit on each line.

Publisher Defaults

Maybe you want to leave all of the decisionmaking to a professional graphic designer. Drag the switch to On to use the formatting recommended by the publisher; you'll see the selections on the menu, but all other options will be grayed out and unavailable.

Brightness

I'm talking here about the illumination of the LCD screen, not the intelligence of the author. Tap the Brightness button and then drag the slider to the right to increase the light level; drag it to the left to decrease it.

A less-bright screen may be more comfortable on your eyes in certain conditions, and a dimmer illumination will use less battery power. Tap outside of the brightness slider to close the menu.

Discover

Here's where your web connection can show off its mind-reading ability. See Figure 3-5. When you tap the Discover button, you'll see three shelves of recommendations that are related to the book you're currently reading:

- **Next in Series.** Other books in the same series by the publisher. For example, choosing a book by Mark Twain published as part of a group of great 19th century literature might also show you titles by Charlotte Bronte and Nathaniel Hawthorne.

- **More by Author.** A listing of other books by the same author as the tome you are currently reading.

- **Customers Who Bought This Also Bought.** And so might you, B&N hopes.

Figure 3-5: B&N would like to suggest more things for you to purchase, in the Discover display.

Reading Books, Magazines, and Newspapers

I'm going way out on a limb here and guess that you'd actually like to do some reading: books, magazines, and newspapers. Good news! That's just about as easy as tapping your finger.

But wait, there's more: You can also make notes about what you're reading. You can highlight favorite passages. You can place multiple bookmarks within the book. And you can share your literary criticism or recommendations with friends using websites like Facebook.

Here are the very basics:

- ✔ Tap any icon that looks like a document (the Home screen, the Library, or file folders) to open the file and let it fill the screen.

- ✔ Tap or swipe to turn pages. (I explain the details in a moment.)

- ✔ The books you read most recently are in the I'm Reading section, but even if they're off that list and back to your Library, you can return to the exact page you last read when you reopen a book.

Opening a book

In Chapter 4 I explain a bit about the book-buying process. But for now, I'm going to make the not-foolish assumption that you have already purchased or downloaded a few titles.

Naturally enough, you begin reading by opening a book. To do that, try any one of these methods:

- ✔ Go to the Home screen and tap any cover on any of the top three panels. Not all books are displayed here, though — just the ones you put on this version of the desktop.

- ✔ Go to the Keep Reading section (on the lower third of the Home screen) to reopen a something you were previously reading.

- ✔ Go to the Library to open the folder (and there you can find books you have purchased or obtained from the Barnes & Noble website, from other online sources, or those that have been brought over to the device from a personal computer or laptop).

Turning the pages

Don't lick your finger and attempt to turn the page; that's unsanitary and will streak the glass. Instead, as shown in Figure 3-6, here's how to move within an electronic book:

    ✔ To turn to the next page, tap anywhere along the right edge of the page.

    ✔ To turn to the next page, swipe to the left; think of this as flicking a page from the right side of an opened book to flip it over. To go forward one page, place your finger on the right side of the page and keep it in contact as you slide it to the left.

    ✔ To turn back to the previous page, tap anywhere along the left edge of the page. Swipe to the right to go to previous pages. To swipe right, place your finger on the left side of the page and slide it to the right (flicking a page, in an electronic way).

    ✔ Use one of the advanced tools. What are they? Read on.

Understanding page numbering

You may see a page number on the screen that corresponds to the printed version of the book (and it could be the hardcover or the paperback). In any case, because the type may be larger than what's in the printed edition, and the screen is smaller than the paper, a single page on your NOOK Tablet may spread across several screens or digital pages. In some designs, you may "turn" page 47 three times before it moves to page 48.

Here's the trick to comparing notes between two eReaders, or between an electronic and a printed copy: Ask for the wording of a particular passage and then find that same passage on your NOOK Tablet by using the Search (also called Find) function.

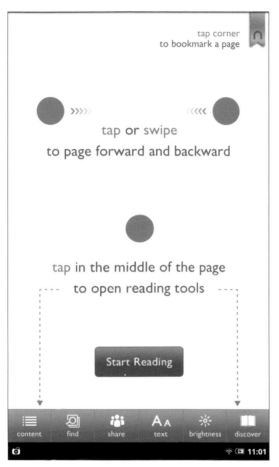

Figure 3-6: Tap or swipe to move forward of backward through the pages of a book.

Adding a bookmark

An electronic bookmark works just like a piece of cardboard between pages: It allows you to quickly open to a particular page. You can set as many bookmarks as you like in each book. See Figure 3-7.

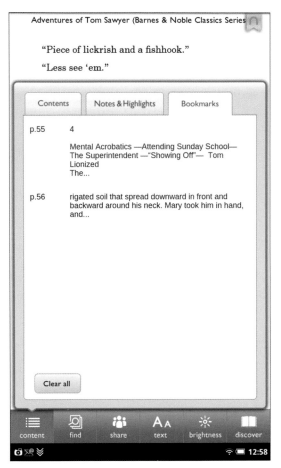

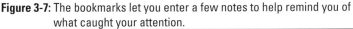

Figure 3-7: The bookmarks let you enter a few notes to help remind you of what caught your attention.

Here's how to handle bookmarks:

- **Set a bookmark on the page you're currently reading.** Tap in the upper-right corner of the page. A small aqua blue ribbon will appear in the corner of the page.

- **List all the bookmarks in a book.** Follow these steps:

1. Tap the center of the page to open the reading tools.

2. Tap the Content icon.

3. Tap the Bookmarks tab (in the Content pane). The tablet will list all the bookmarks in the book.

✔ **Tap a bookmark** in the list to jump directly to the passage or page.

✔ **Close the bookmark list without visiting a bookmark.** Tap anywhere on the book page outside the list of bookmarks.

✔ **Remove a bookmark on the current page.** Tap the blue ribbon in the upper-right corner of the page to make it go away.

✔ **Clear all the bookmarks in a book:**

   1. Tap the Content icon in the reading tools.

   2. Tap the Bookmarks tab.

   3. Tap the Clear All button.

   4. Tap OK.

Selecting text for sharing or definition

What exactly is a battologist? I mean, really, *what exactly is a battologist?* If you come across a weird word, look it up in the built-in copy of the *Merriam-Webster's Collegiate Dictionary,* Eleventh Edition. But if that dictionary can't help you answer the question, "What exactly is a battologist?" then go out on the web to consult other resources. See Figure 3-8. The answer to "What exactly is a battologist?" by the way, is: someone who unnecessarily repeats something.

You can share a word (like you-know-what), or pick up a short passage and send it by e-mail (or Twitter or in a Facebook post). The NOOK Tablet is ready, willing, and able to assist.

words. Word origins not only shed light on their current meaning, but offer clues to their ...

Obsolete Word of the Day: **battologist**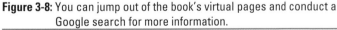
obsoleteword.blogspot.com/2007/08/**battologist**.html
Aug 28, 2007 – **battologist**. This is someone who repeats the same thing for no reason. It comes from the Greek word for stammerer. posted by the scribbler ...

Battologist - definition of **Battologist** by the Free Online Dictionary ...
www.thefreedictionary.com/**Battologist**
Legal dictionary. Financial dictionary. Acronyms. Idioms. Encyclopedia. Wikipedia encyclopedia ? **Battologist**. 0.01 sec. Bat´tol´o·gist. n. 1. One who battologizes. ...

battologist - Encyclopedia
www.encyclo.co.uk/define/**battologist**
battologist - Meaning and definition. ... Look up: **battologist**. **Battologist** Bat·tol'o· gist noun One who battologizes. Found on http:// www.encyclo.co.uk/webster/B/23 ...

Battologist...Are You One? | | CF Web ProfessionalsCF Web Professionals
www.cfwebprofessionals.com/blog/general/**battologist**-are-you-one/
Oct 30, 2010 – I was surfing the web this morning, for now I can't remember what – when I ran into the word: **battologist**. It piqued my interest. ...

the **battologist** - YouTube
www.youtube.com/watch?v=hVnW3lSeb2Q
Aug 10, 2010 - 8 min - Uploaded by violettemaschine
Our annual entry into the 48 Hour Film Project-Denver! This was the first year I was director of ...
More videos for **battologist** »

battologist's Music Profile – Users at Last.fm
www.last.fm/user/**battologist**

Figure 3-8: You can jump out of the book's virtual pages and conduct a Google search for more information.

To select a word, press and hold on a word and then lift your finger. The word will be highlighted in a yellow block, and you'll see a blue vertical bar on either side of it. (Unless, of course, you have chosen a different color theme for the page, in which case other colors will be applied.)

✔ To expand the highlight from a single word to a passage, tap and then drag one of the vertical bars. When you lift your finger or fingers (you can use your thumb and pointing finger to cover more area), the Text Selection toolbar appears.

✔ You can't directly print a passage from your NOOK Tablet (at least not in the initial release), but here's what you can do: Select a passage and send it to yourself by e-mail. Then use a computer and printer to make a hard copy.

Be sure you understand the proper use of citations if you are using part of a copyrighted book in an academic paper or a publication of your own.

Picking the Text Selection Toolbar

The Text Selection Toolbar has these options:

✔ **Highlight.** Mark a single word or a passage in a block of color.

✔ **Notes.** Insert a comment (up to 512 characters) about the highlighted word or phrase; the date and time are included. A small icon, like a sticky note, will appear along the margin and you can search for what's in your note later on. You can view and change notes any time. You can also make them invisible. Why? Perhaps you want to share a selection or loan a book to someone but keep your comments private. See Figure 3-9.

  • **View All Notes.** Tap the page to display the reading tools. Tap Content. Tap the Notes & Highlights tab.

  • **Edit a Note.** Tap the Note icon you want to edit; it appears onscreen. Choose Edit and use the keyboard to make changes. Tap the Post button.

  • **Remove a Note.** Tap the highlighted word or phrase. Tap Remove Note.

  • **Make Notes Visible or Invisible.** Tap the page to display Reading Tools. Tap the Content icon. Tap the Notes & Highlights tab. Slide the On/Off switch labeled Notes & Highlights to the setting you want.

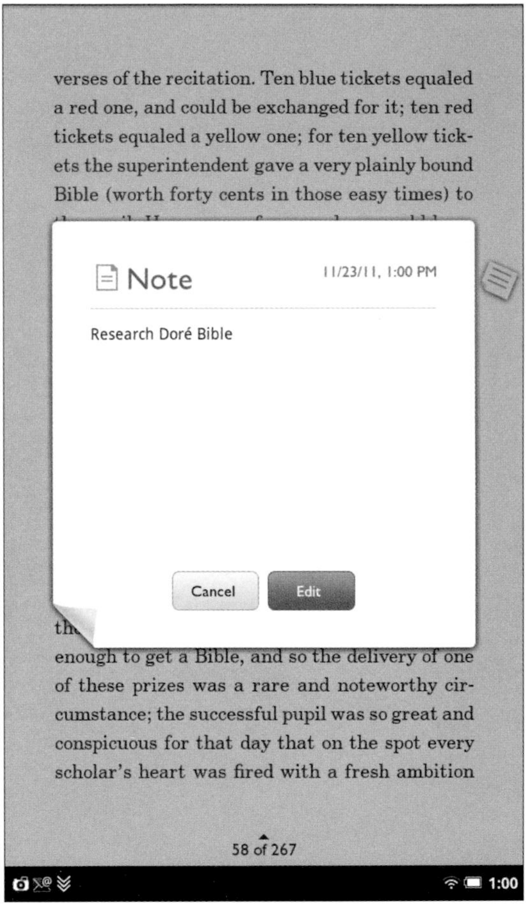

verses of the recitation. Ten blue tickets equaled
a red one, and could be exchanged for it; ten red
tickets equaled a yellow one; for ten yellow tickets the superintendent gave a very plainly bound
Bible (worth forty cents in those easy times) to

▤ **Note**   11/23/11, 1:00 PM

Research Doré Bible

[Cancel] [Edit]

enough to get a Bible, and so the delivery of one
of these prizes was a rare and noteworthy cir-
cumstance; the successful pupil was so great and
conspicuous for that day that on the spot every
scholar's heart was fired with a fresh ambition

58 of 267

Figure 3-9: Create a book note as a reminder of something important or a
task you want to perform.

- **Change the Highlighting Color for a Note.** Tap the
  highlighted word or phrase in the passage associated with a note. Tap the highlighting color you
  want to use.

✔ **Share.** When you tap the Share icon, a submenu offers
  you the choice to pass along your insights or the words
  you've selected. The quotes are limited to about 350
  characters. Here's how to share:

- **Contacts.** Choose one or more e-mail contacts to send the material to. If you haven't set up contacts or need to expand the listing, tap the Add Contacts button to fill in a form with a name and e-mail address.

- **On Facebook.** Post a quote and a short message on your own Facebook wall or on a Facebook friend's wall.

- **Via Twitter.** Post a short quote (limited to <140 characters) using your pre-established Twitter account. At the lower right, a number tells you how many characters you have left; a negative number means you're over 140.

✔ **Look Up.** Search for a word's meaning. To use Wikipedia or Google search, you need a working WiFi Internet connection.

- **In the Dictionary.** Tap the Look Up icon and a pop-up window will display the meaning, if one is available. To close the window, tap anywhere outside the window.

- **In Wikipedia or in a Google search.** Tap the Look Up icon; the pop-up window appears with a dictionary definition (if available). Tap the Google icon to search, or tap the golfball-like Wikipedia icon to look there.

✔ **Find.** Tap the Find button to search the entire book or document. All instances of the word or phrase are highlighted and displayed in a box; jump to any of them by touching their entry. You may be reading an unsearchable PDF.

Searching in a book

In most eBooks you can search for a particular word or phrase. However, if you're using a public domain file that is just a picture of pages (rather than the actual text), searching is impossible.

The Find function, shown in Figure 3-10, can hunt through the text of a publication for a word or phrase. Here's how to search:

1. **In the Reading Tools menu, tap the Find button.**

2. **Tap a previous query or type a new search.**

3. **Tap Done.**

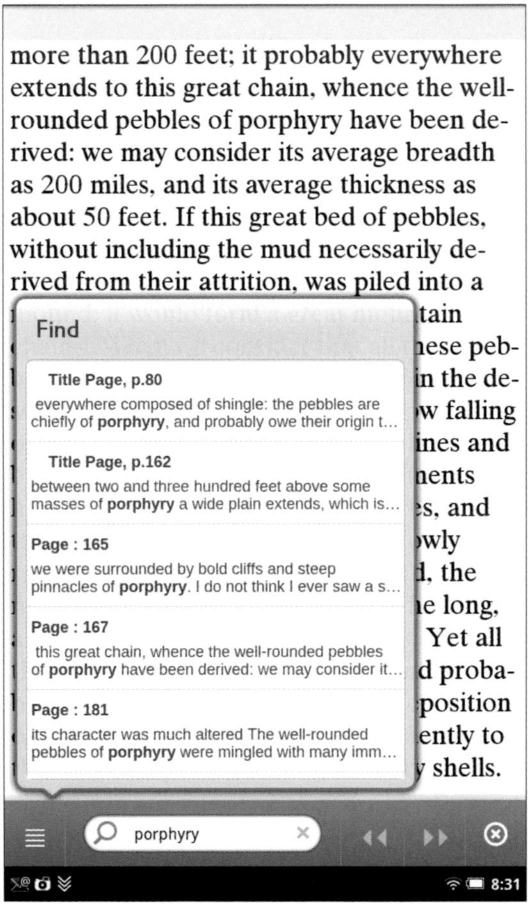

more than 200 feet: it probably everywhere extends to this great chain, whence the well-rounded pebbles of porphyry have been derived: we may consider its average breadth as 200 miles, and its average thickness as about 50 feet. If this great bed of pebbles, without including the mud necessarily derived from their attrition, was piled into a

Find

Title Page, p.80
everywhere composed of shingle: the pebbles are chiefly of **porphyry**, and probably owe their origin t...

Title Page, p.162
between two and three hundred feet above some masses of **porphyry** a wide plain extends, which is...

Page : 165
we were surrounded by bold cliffs and steep pinnacles of **porphyry**. I do not think I ever saw a s...

Page : 167
this great chain, whence the well-rounded pebbles of **porphyry** have been derived: we may consider it...

Page : 181
its character was much altered The well-rounded pebbles of **porphyry** were mingled with many imm...

porphyry

8:31

Figure 3-10: Entering a word or phrase into the Find box allows the tablet to hunt through the current document.

Customizing the Search tool

You can broaden or narrow your searches. You can individually select most of the places to look for a file. And you can also clear your history of recent searches (another way to protect your privacy on some level). When you use it from the quick nav bar, the Search tool always looks in your NOOK Tablet Library; if you're connected by WiFi to www.BN.com, it also looks for titles in the online shop. You can include or exclude other areas.

To change the places your NOOK Tablet will look, go to the Searchable Items screen shown in Figure 3-11:

1. **Press the ∩ button to display the quick nav bar.**

2. **Tap the Settings button.**

3. **On the Settings screen, tap Search (in the App Settings section).**

   The Search Settings screen is displayed.

4. **Tap Searchable Items.**

   A check box shows up by all the areas you can search; the Library and Shop are grayed out because you can't remove them from searches.

Reading a magazine

Magazines come in all shapes, sizes, and special designs. Digital formats vary greatly; the way you see pages from a periodical using the NOOK Tablet may be different from one magazine to another and some may have interactive features.

Most magazines comes in two views. You get to choose:

✔ **Page view** shows the entire page, including text and images.

✔ **Article view** shows text only. See Figure 3-12.

Figure 3-11: Your selections determine where the NOOK Tablet searches for a word or phrase.

Page view

This digital representation of the printed magazine has photographs, drawings, charts, and other elements. You'll see small images in the lower half of the screen. Page view is available in both portrait and landscape modes.

Figure 3-12: Try Page view in a spectacular magazine like *National Geographic.*

✔ To move through the magazine, swipe your finger along the thumbnail images.

✔ Tap a page to jump directly to it; a progress bar below the images shows where you are in the entire issue.

✔ As you read a page, tap the right side of the screen to move to the next page; tap the left side to go back a page.

Why is navigating a magazine different than navigating a book? Good question. Magazine publishers use a different electronic design than book publishers.

✔ To make the thumbnail images reappear, tap in the middle of the screen.

Article view

This format shows articles with few (or no) illustrations or photos. You can scroll through the text as you would in a book. See Figure 3-13.

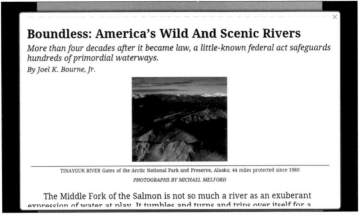

Boundless: America's Wild And Scenic Rivers

More than four decades after it became law, a little-known federal act safeguards hundreds of primordial waterways.

By Joel K. Bourne, Jr.

TINAYGUK RIVER Gates of the Arctic National Park and Preserve, Alaska; 44 miles protected since 1980

PHOTOGRAPHS BY MICHAEL MELFORD

The Middle Fork of the Salmon is not so much a river as an exuberant expression of water at play. It tumbles and turns and trips over itself for a

Figure 3-13: Article view emphasizes the text of a magazine piece; you can always go back to page view to enjoy photographs and illustrations.

Content navigation

You can also go directly from article to article:

1. **Tap the center of the screen.**
2. **Tap the Content icon at the bottom of the page.**

   A window opens.
3. **Tap the cover, table of contents, or specific article.**

Reading a newspaper

Whether you've downloaded a single issue or you subscribe, newspapers are on your Daily Shelf and on the Newsstand page of your Library.

✓ To open a newspaper, tap its front page. When it opens, the front page shows headlines and one or two paragraphs from the start of major articles.

✓ To read an article in more depth, tap its headline or the introductory paragraphs.

✔ To share parts of an article, tap in the middle of the page. From the reading tools, choose Share or Notes (if the publisher has allowed those features).

✔ Bookmark a page by tapping in the upper-right corner of the page.

✔ To turn to the next page of a newspaper, do any of the following:

- Tap along the right edge of the screen.
- Swipe your finger from right to left across the screen.
- Swipe your finger from low to high on the screen.

✔ To go back a page in a newspaper, do one of these actions:

- Tap along the left edge of the screen.
- Swipe your finger from left to right across the screen.
- Swipe your finger from high to low on the screen.

Reading for Kids of All Ages

The NOOK Tablet offers some special features for young readers (and those of us who sit by their side as they discover the joys of reading) with special features that are part of the NOOK Kids picture books. Some children's books have a bit of animation that you can set into motion by tapping the screen; others read aloud parts of the book. See Figure 3-14.

Children's books open in landscape mode to better present the two-page spreads of most picture books. You may find the speaker tough to hear in noisy situations; one solution is to use *two* sets of earphones plugged into a simple splitter attached to the tablet's audio output. Splitters are available at most electronics stores and shacks.

Long ago, elephants had no trunks. They had only blackish, bulgy noses as big as boots. Their noses were suitable for sniffing and for wriggling side to side—but absolutely useless for picking things up.

In these far off times, there was one Elephant's Child in Africa who was born with endless curiosity. He asked ever-so-many questions, which got him in ever-so-much trouble!

Figure 3-14: A book for kids of all ages.

Manipulate with these tips, too:

- ✔ To make text bigger, double-tap it to enlarge it. Double-tap to return to the original size and position.

- ✔ To make text bigger, zoom in by pinching in on the image and text.

- ✔ Drag an image to move it around on the page.

Moving from page to page

Follow these steps:

- ✔ Swipe to the left (drag your finger from right to left across the screen) to go forward.

- ✔ Tap anywhere on the right edge of the screen.

- ✔ To go backwards in the book, swipe to the right or tap the left side.

Skipping part of a children's book

To go from one part of a kid's book to another, follow these steps:

1. **Tap the white arrow at the bottom of the screen.**

   Small pages from the book appear.

2. **Slide your finger across the images.**

3. **Tap the small image of the page you want to read.**

Choosing a reading style

Some children's books can narrate. Others move. These special features appear only if the book includes them. See Figure 3-15.

Figure 3-15: Some NOOK Kids books include prerecorded audio tracks, or you may be able to add your own.

Read by Myself

Just the words and pictures. Tap the blue button to open the book. Some special activities may be marked with a white star; tap the star to play. Better yet, let a kid tap the star.

Read to Me or Read and Play

Read and Play books have audio tracks, and interactive features, marked with a white star. Tap the orange Read to Me, or the purple Read and Play buttons to hear the author or an actor read aloud.

If you're enjoying a Read and Play book, you can only turn the pages by tapping the onscreen arrows. The pages won't turn if you tap them.

Read and Record

Daddy or Mommy (or a child!) can become the voice of a book. Here's how:

1. **Tap the cover of a kid's book that has the Read and Record feature.**

2. **On the opening screen, tap the green Read and Record button.**

   The book opens to the first page.

3. **Tap the green Read and Record button.**

   It will change to a Stop button. But don't stop.

4. **Start reading.**

   Here are some tips:

   - The tiny hole on the right side of the NOOK Tablet is the microphone. Don't cover it with your hand while you're recording.

   - Hold the tablet about 15 inches away from your mouth.

   - Try to record in a quiet place without background noise.

5. **When you're done recording, tap the Stop button.**

Keep these general recording tips in mind:

   ✓ If you'd like to hear your recording right away, press the Play button. Press the Pause button when you're done listening.

✔ If you're a perfectionist (or if someone dropped a pile of plates while the microphone was on), press the Re-record button to do it again.

✔ To keep recording, swipe or tap to the next page and then tap the Record button.

✔ To end a recording session at any time, tap the Done button in the lower left. A screen asks you to choose a picture as a symbol. Type a name for the recording.

✔ To play a recording, open the book and tap the picture icon for the file you created.

✔ To re-record, change the name, or delete the audio file, tap the Edit button next to the picture icon and then choose the option you want.

The recording you make is saved in the My Files folder; they aren't part of the NOOK Kids book itself. When you connect your NOOK Tablet to a desktop or laptop computer, you can make a copy of the file there, or move it to the microSD/SDHC memory card you may have installed in the tablet.

Studying a NOOK Comics Book

Pow! Ooph! Wow! The NOOK Tablet can display specially formatted NOOK comics in portrait or landscape mode. Moving within a NOOK Comics book is very similar to the steps involved in NOOK Kids titles.

✔ Tap the cover of a comic book to open it. See Figure 3-16.

✔ Swipe left or right to go forward or back, or tap the right or left side of the page for the same effect.

✔ Tap in the center of the screen to bring up the reader tools, including small versions of the entire document. Tap any image to go directly to a particular page.

✔ To zoom in on text and images, double-tap or use the pinch-out gesture. Double-tap again to return the page to normal.

✔ Bookmark a page by tapping the + icon in the upper right. Once you place a marker, tap the center of the page to display reader tools, tap the Content icon, and then tap the Bookmarks tab.

✔ Jump directly to any bookmarked page by tapping the bookmark.

Figure 3-16: Betty and Veronica never looked so good as they do in NOOK comics.

Side-Loading Files

You can download this and that over the Internet via your WiFi connection from your NOOK Tablet to a wireless router. But you can bring files to a NOOK Tablet by side-loading, too. *Side-loading* means moving a copy of a file from your laptop or personal computer to your NOOK Tablet using the USB cable that comes with the device (or an identical replacement cable).

Use only the USB cable provided with your NOOK Tablet or an exact duplicate. There are many different types of USB cables and using the wrong one could damage the physical connector and cause tablet troubles.

What kind of files can you side-load onto a NOOK Tablet? There are two answers, so I'll give you both:

- ✔ You can store any compatible audio, video, picture, text, spreadsheet, presentation, or book file on your NOOK Tablet and use it to play them back. The NOOK Tablet can read the following file types:

  - **EPUB.** The default format for books.

  - **PDF.** Another format used for some books and publications, and for things like catalogs, instruction manuals, and documents.

  - **Word.** Microsoft Office text files in doc, docx, docm, dot, dotx, and dotm formats.

  - **Excel.** Microsoft Office spreadsheet files in xls, xlsx, xlsm, xlt, xltx, and xltm formats.

  - **PowerPoint.** Microsoft Office presentation files in ppt, pptx, pptm, pps, ppsx, ppsm, pot, potx, and potm formats. (Special effects including animations, transitions, and multi-image slides will not show those features on the tablet.) See Figure 3-17.

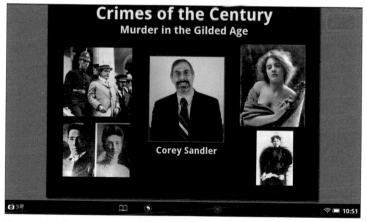

Figure 3-17: You can work with basic PowerPoint functions; advanced animations and transitions aren't yet supported.

- **Plain text.** Unformatted text from many sources, stored as a txt file.

- **Web pages.** Material stored using HTML, stored as htm, html, or xhtml files.

- **Comic book archive.** One great leap for man (and womankind): an advanced scheme for comic books, stored using the cbz format.

- **Music, video, and image files.** You know of what I speak.

- **Music and audio.** The NOOK Tablet can play files in any of these formats: aac, amr, mid, midi, mp3, m4a, ogg, or wav.

- **Video.** The tablet can play media files as large as 2GB, in any of these formats: Adobe Flash, 3gp, 3g2, mkv, mp4, or m4v.

- **Images.** The preferred format is jpg.

✔ You can place any kind of electronic file — including formats that won't work on the tablet— as if the tablet were an external hard drive. I sometimes do exactly that, storing files I may need on a business trip, with the expectation of side-loading them onto a desktop or laptop computer if I need to use them.

As delivered, the NOOK Table can open and display or play any of the file formats I have listed. The facility, though, is read-only; you can't edit or change them. However, you can buy apps through www.BN.com that let you do some basic Microsoft Office editing.

Always keep backup copies of important files on your personal computer. That's true even if you use your NOOK Tablet as a backup device for some of your files when you travel. For example, if you're traveling to give a presentation, you can store copies of PowerPoint and Word files on the device as a second copy in case your laptop fails or disappears.

Moving files from a computer to your NOOK Tablet

To transfer files from your personal computer to your NOOK Tablet, do this:

1. **Turn on your Windows-based or Macintosh personal computer.**

   Allow it to fully get ready.

2. **Turn on your NOOK Tablet.**

   It's faster to the starting line than a big computer, but then again, it's not a big computer.

3. **Connect the small end of the USB cable that came with your NOOK to the Tablet.**

4. **Connect the larger end of the USB cable to a USB port on your personal computer.**

   After a few moments, your computer should say it has detected a new disk drive. Depending on your computer, the drive may show up as MyNOOK, or it may just be an extra drive. There will be a second entry for the microSD/SDHC memory slot. If your computer has one internal hard drive plus a CD/DVD drive, the NOOK may show up as Removable Disk E: and Removable Drive F.

   Some Windows computers may ask if you want to install a driver for a NOOK device. Click Cancel to close this dialog box.

5. **On your computer, click the NOOK drive to open it.**

6. **Click My Files to open that subfolder.**

7. **Drag and drop files from the computer to the right subfolder.**

   Here are the folders on the NOOK Tablet:

   - Books
   - Documents

- Magazines
- Music
- My Downloads
- Newspapers
- NOOK Kids Recordings
- Pictures
- Videos
- Wallpapers

In most cases, it doesn't matter where you place a particular type of file because the NOOK Tablet will sort it out for you. Files in picture format will appear in the gallery; videos will appear in the video player. But it does make your NOOK Tablet nicely organized. And one more thing: You can create your own folder on the tablet, using the Make Folder (or equivalent) command on your computer, and use it to store files of your choice.

Preparing files for the NOOK Tablet

What if you have files on your desktop or laptop computer that you want to use on your NOOK Tablet, but the files are stored in the wrong format? In most cases, you can use a program or utility on your computer to convert the files to a compatible format.

For example, any file you can open in Microsoft Office can be saved in one of the formats that the NOOK can display; just use the Save As command and select the proper format. The same process can be used to convert photos or drawings to JPG format, using a graphics program such as Adobe Photoshop, Adobe Photoshop Elements, or a Macintosh image editor.

When you process an image for the NOOK Tablet, consider resizing it. Set the image to about 4 x 6 inches. The resolution can be set at 72 or 96 dpi. Choose Save As, select JPG, and type a new name. That way you don't lose the original larger, higher-resolution file.

Ejecting the NOOK Tablet from a computer

When you connect your NOOK to a laptop or desktop computer, the device becomes the equivalent of an extra hard disk drive — extra storage. To protect against damaging the files that you copy to the tablet, you should *eject* the device before you physically unplug the USB cable. (The official instructions say this is a "must do." I classify it as a "should do." In any case, I know I do do that old voodoo that I do so well, because a corrupted file is not pretty.)

You can eject the NOOK by

- Clicking the Eject button. (You might see instructions onscreen.)

- Using the operating system (described in the following sections).

Windows-based computer or laptop

Follow these steps:

1. **Open the My Computer (or Computer) folder.**

2. **Click the icon for the Removable Drive for the NOOK Tablet.**

   Click it just once with the left mouse button.

3. **Right-click the Removable Drive icon.**

   A submenu appears.

4. **Click Eject.**

5. **If a microSDHC card is in your NOOK Tablet, repeat Steps 1–4.**

6. **Unplug the USB cable from the computer.**

   You can unplug the cable from the tablet or leave it attached if you'll connect again to the computer soon. After the tablet is ejected and you remove the USB cable from the computer, the tablet tells you that it's processing any new files. Give it a moment to put books and documents on the shelf.

Here is a second way to eject a NOOK Tablet from a Windows-based machine:

1. **On the taskbar at the bottom of the Windows screen, click the Safely Remove Hardware icon.**

   You should see something like, "Safely remove USB mass storage device- Drive *x*."

2. **Choose based on your situation:**

   - If only one device is attached, then this is your NOOK Tablet. Go to Step 3.

   - If more than one device is attached, choose the drive letter assigned to the NOOK Tablet.

3. **Click the item in the pop-up notice.**

   The system should respond with "Safe to remove hardware."

4. **If a microSDHC card is in your NOOK Tablet, repeat Steps 1–3.**

5. **Unplug the USB cable from the computer.**

   You can also unplug the cable from the tablet or leave it attached if you intend to connect again to the computer soon.

Macintosh computer or laptop

Follow these steps:

1. **Open the Finder and select the drive for the NOOK Tablet.**

2. **From the File menu, select Eject.**

3. **If a microSD or microSDHC card is in your NOOK Tablet, eject that memory card.**

4. **Unplug the USB cable from the computer.**

   You can also unplug the cable from the reader or leave it attached if you intend to connect again to the computer soon.

Traveling Abroad with a NOOK Tablet

Nothing prevents you from taking your NOOK Tablet outside of the United States, although some roadblocks keep you from buying something when you're in another country. Why? Because most publisher-author contracts restrict selling a book in foreign countries (or indicate varying royalty rates).

Here's a guide to the international lay of the land:

- ✔ You can read anything that's already on your NOOK Tablet as you travel anywhere in the world.

- ✔ As of the end of 2011, NOOK Tablet devices are only being sold to people who have a billing address in the United States or one of its territories.

- ✔ You can only buy content for your tablet if you have a billing address in the United States, U.S. territories, or Canada. You must make the purchase while you are (or your tablet is) physically within the United States, its territories, and Canada. (The device will identify its location through its WiFi router.)

- ✏ You can download items you've already bought from anywhere in the world where you can obtain a WiFi signal.

- ✏ You can lend and borrow eBooks from anywhere in the world.

- ✏ Periodicals are automatically downloaded to your NOOK Tablet anywhere you can connect to a WiFi system.

- ✏ It's tough to get foreign and foreign-language eBooks for the NOOK Tablet. This restriction doesn't apply to books in the public domain; check for titles there.

- ✏ The NOOK Tablet can display several foreign languages, and other languages are possible if the typefaces are embedded in the eBook files.

Oh, and one more thing: The battery recharger for your NOOK Tablet has prongs that connect to wall outlets in the United States and Canada. It *can* work with power from about 110 to 240 volts. You need a plug adapter if you want to use the NOOK Tablet in a country that uses plugs of other shapes. You *don't* need to convert or reduce the voltage — just change the shape of the plug.

Chapter 4

Stocking Shelves and Adding Apps

*M*an — and woman — cannot live on bread alone. We also need great books. It's not pretty to own a perfectly capable tablet and not have it stocked with books, magazines, newspapers, and the occasional comic book.

In this chapter you explore ways to fill those shelves with bestsellers, literary classics, dozens of *For Dummies* books, and obscure research material of interest only to you. I will also tell you how to find free eBooks. You also read about how to download apps so you can expand the capabilities of your NOOK Tablet.

For most of this chapter, I talk about Barnes & Noble and www.BN.com because it's the prime seller of the NOOK Tablet and because you can easily get to its store by tapping the Store icon on your tablet. However, nearly all of the other online booksellers are similar.

Welcome B&N Shoppers!

The first time you turn on your NOOK Tablet, devote a few minutes to basic setup. You're offered a short video about NOOK Tablet features. Then come the formalities:

- Accepting the terms of service (TOS). You *have* to accept the terms of service in order to use the NOOK Tablet. There's nothing out of the ordinary in the terms, other than turning over all rights to your next bestselling Great American Novel, your dog or cat, and your most comfortable pair of shoes. (Actually, they left all of that stuff out.)

- Setting the current time and time zone. Again, you've got to make sure you get this right.

- Registering your NOOK Tablet to a Barnes & Noble account. This lets your tablet get to any eBooks and periodicals already in your account, and it lets you shop for new ones. You can set up a B&N account two ways:

  - Directly from the NOOK Tablet, using a WiFi link to the Internet.

  - From a desktop or laptop computer, connecting to the Internet by cable, wire, or WiFi.

In addition to the eReader on the NOOK Tablet, Barnes & Noble offers free software that lets you read (and buy) publications on devices including desktop and laptop PCs, Macintoshes, iPads, iPhones, and various Android devices.

However you set up your B&N account, registration has to be done using the WiFi connection; there are no ifs, ands, or wires about it. So here are your options:

- Configure your NOOK Tablet at a Barnes & Noble store; you'll find a free and open WiFi system specifically aimed at you.

- Use a WiFi system at home, work, school, library, or café. In nearly all of these situations you need a login and password from the system owner or administrator (or the person behind the counter).

After you set up an account, here's how to go to the store from your NOOK Tablet:

1. **Make sure you have a working WiFi connection to the Internet.**

2. **Tap the Sign In button.**

3. **Enter the e-mail address and password for your account.**

4. **Tap Submit.**

After you link your NOOK to your account, you don't have to do it again. That link is protected behind the password you have to enter to use the tablet. I strongly suggest that you do that. I explain in the very next section.

Once you start using your NOOK Tablet, *synchronization* (or syncing) takes place in the background — you don't have to do anything. You can request an update while a wireless connection is established. Do this by tapping the Sync icon (a pair of arrows chasing each other around in a circle) on the Library page.

Locking Things Down

Please allow me to ask a few questions:

- ✔ Will you ever loan your NOOK Tablet to someone else?

- ✔ Will anyone (family, friends, acquaintances, or perfect strangers) ever have access to your NOOK Tablet when you're not around?

- ✔ Can you conceive the possibility that your NOOK Tablet might someday (perish the thought) be lost or stolen?

If the answer to any of these questions is Yes or Maybe, I recommend creating a password and making anyone who's going to buy something enter that password. Make it a pretty tough password, too. The best password is so complex and unobvious that no one can guess it. My favorite type of password is a phone number or an address that has no direct connection to you but which you can recall from memory. Oh, and don't write it down on a sticky note applied to the bottom of the NOOK Tablet.

Requiring a password to make purchases

To configure your NOOK Tablet to require a password for purchases:

1. **Press the ∩ button to display the quick nav bar.**

2. **Tap the Settings button.**

3. **On the Settings screen, tap Shop.**

   It's in the App Settings section.

4. **Tap the check box next to Require Password for Purchases.**

   If the check box is bold, rather than grayed out, the option is already turned on; you don't need to tap it.

5. **In the dialog box that appears, type your B&N account password.**

6. **Tap OK.**

Removing the requirement for a password to make purchases

If your tablet asks for a password when someone tries to buy something, but you want to remove that requirement, here's how to unring that bell. Follow Steps 1 through 4 from the process for "Requiring a password to make purchases." Then continue as follows:

1. **Press the ∩ button to display the quick nav bar.**

2. **Tap the Settings button.**

3. **On the Settings screen, tap Shop.**

   It's in the App Settings section.

4. **In the dialog box that appears, type the password.**

5. **Tap the check box next to Require Password for Purchases.**

6. **Tap OK.**

Shopping on Your NOOK Tablet

The bottom line, of course, is that without books, magazines, videos, music, apps, or document files, your NOOK Tablet is simply a fancy way to play Sudoku. You're going to want to fill it up. See Figure 4-1. Here's how to shop in the B&N Store:

1. **Press the ∩ button to display the quick nav bar.**

2. **Tap the Shop button.**

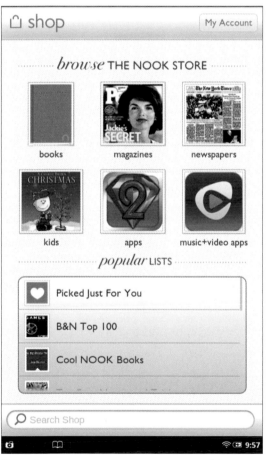

Figure 4-1: You can browse the changing NOOK store by category or list.

Just as you do when you walk into a brick-and-mortar book-store, you have to make your way past promotions for new titles and specials. What you see today is likely to be different from what you saw yesterday or will find tomorrow. Here are some typical offerings for browsing:

- **Books.** Choose from romance, mystery, crime, science fiction, biography, memoir, business and personal finance, history, humor . . . think of it as strolling the aisles of a store. Also included in the book department: comics.

- **Magazines.** Choose *Cosmopolitan* to *Maxim*, from *National Geographic* to *Southern Living*, from *Bon Appetit* to *Fitness Magazine*. In most cases, you can buy one issue or subscribe.

- **Newspapers.** Choose from *The New York Times, Financial Times,* and *The Onion.* You'll find not just national papers but also regional publications.

- **Kids.** Several hundred books (picture and chapter) are there for pre-readers through teens. Included are Read and Play Books, which add narration, sound effects, and interactive features. Chapter 3 tells more about kids' books.

- **Apps.** A growing selection of small programs (apps) is what you find here. B&N says it wants to concentrate on book-related apps as well as carefully selected games and utilities for people on the go.

- **Music+Video Apps.** This special section of apps is sup-posed to enhance audio and video on the NOOK Tablet.

In addition, you can go through Popular Lists to find things like the B&N Top 100, *The New York Times* bestsellers, and new releases. Again, these lists change over time and include things like seasonal specials (Christmas, Mother's Day, Father's Day, and the like). Tap any of the lists to explore. To read more about a suggestion, double-tap the cover.

Searching for a specific book

As much as I love to browse the aisles (physical or electronic) of a good bookstore, sometimes I know exactly what I want. See Figure 4-2.

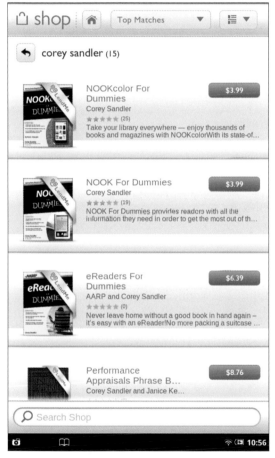

Figure 4-2: You can search by author name, subject, or title. The B&N store comes up with a customized list.

To search for a particular book or periodical:

1. **Tap the Search Shop field at the bottom of the Shop screen.**

   The virtual onscreen keyboard appears.

2. **Type the title, author, or subject you're looking for.**

   You don't have to distinguish between a title, author, or subject. The search engine will sort through all of the possibilities.

3. **Tap the Search button.**

   Scroll through the results by dragging your finger up or down. A green button shows the prices on the B&N site. If you see a gray Purchased label, you already bought that title for the current account; once you've paid, you can always download it again.

Buying a book

Find a book you want. Here's what else to do:

1. **Tap the cover to see its details.**

   Sometimes you can see a sample from the book — an entire chapter or a hop, skip, and jump through the pages. See Figure 4-3.

   Tap the Share button to tell people what you've found. (Perhaps you'd like to drop a hint about the perfect birthday gift for you?) You can rate and review your thoughts about the title, posting them to Facebook or Twitter.

2. **Tap the green button that shows the price.**

   The button will change its label to Confirm.

3. **Tap the Confirm button.**

   Your credit card is charged; the book starts coming to your tablet; a progress bar shows you how much has arrived. (If a download is interrupted because of a problem with the wireless connection or other causes, it will automatically resume the next time it gets a chance.) The new item appears on the left of the Daily Shelf and in your Library. And it wears a New badge until you open it.

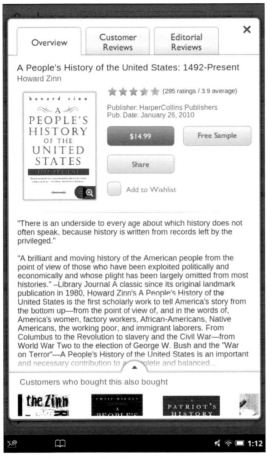

Figure 4-3: A book's details page lets you access a sample (in some books) and the all-important green (Buy Me Now) button.

If you're asking to download a copy of a free book at the Barnes & Noble store, you still go through the "purchase" process; the cost will register as $0. If you pre-order an eBook, you're charged when it's officially published.

Buying magazines or newspapers

You can buy individual issues of a newspaper or magazine, or subscribe to daily, weekly, or monthly delivery of the periodical. Just as in the world of paper and ink, the best deals come with longer-term subscriptions. Once you buy, the first issue downloads immediately; see Figure 4-4.

Nearly every magazine and newspaper offers free 14-day trials; you can get one free trial for each publication. If you cancel the subscription before the end of the trial, your credit card isn't charged. Otherwise, deliveries continue and your credit card is charged automatically at the monthly subscription rate. To cancel a periodical subscription, go to your account at www.BN.com, log in, and go to the Manage Subscriptions section.

Buying a single issue

To buy a single issue, follow these steps:

1. **Tap the cover and open the Details page.**
2. **Tap the Buy Current Issue button.**
3. **Tap Confirm.**

    The issue downloads.

4. **Tap the Read button.**

Subscribing to a periodical

The subscription process begins with a free trial; if you don't cancel before the end of the trial, you are automatically subscribed. See Figure 4-5.

1. **Tap the cover and open the Details page.**
2. **Tap the Free Trial button.**
3. **Tap Confirm.**
4. **Tap the Start My Free Trial button.**

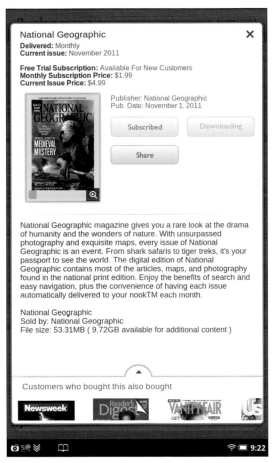

National Geographic   ✕
Delivered: Monthly
Current issue: November 2011

Free Trial Subscription: Available For New Customers
Monthly Subscription Price: $1.99
Current Issue Price: $4.99

Publisher: National Geographic
Pub. Date: November 1, 2011

[Subscribed]   [Downloading]

[Share]

National Geographic magazine gives you a rare look at the drama
of humanity and the wonders of nature. With unsurpassed
photography and exquisite maps, every issue of National
Geographic is an event. From shark safaris to tiger treks, it's your
passport to see the world. The digital edition of National
Geographic contains most of the articles, maps, and photography
found in the national print edition. Enjoy the benefits of search and
easy navigation, plus the convenience of having each issue
automatically delivered to your nookTM each month.

National Geographic
Sold by: National Geographic
File size: 53.31MB (9.72GB available for additional content)

Customers who bought this also bought

Figure 4-4: A small green bar shows how far along a magazine download
has gotten. This issue is completely downloaded.

You can always return to the Shop page by tapping the Shop
icon in the upper-left corner of the screen.

Paying the bill

Unless you say otherwise, your credit card is charged when
you buy something from Barnes & Noble. It's all done for you;
there are no receipts to sign.

The New York Times ✕

Delivered: Daily
Current issue: November 22, 2011

Free Trial Subscription: Available For New Customers
Monthly Subscription Price: $19.99
Current Issue Price: $0.99

Publisher: New York Times
Pub. Date: November 22, 2011

[Free Trial] [Buy Current Issue]

[Share]

[ ] Add to Wishlist

The New York Times is dedicated to providing news coverage of exceptional depth and breadth, as well as opinion that is thoughtful and stimulating. Widely quoted and published since 1851, The New York Times is regarded by many as the nation's pre-eminent newspaper.

This digital edition of The New York Times contains the articles found in the print edition, but omits some images and tables. Also, features such as the crossword puzzle, box scores and classifieds are not currently available.

Additional Benefit:
All active subscriptions to The New York Times through NOOK Newsstand include access to NYTimes.com, The Times's award-winning website, including timely news updates, opinions, blogs, video, interactive graphics and more! NOOK Newsstand subscribers to The New York Times will receive instructions via email on how to access NYTim   m.

Customers who bought this also bought

🖰   📖   🛜 🔋 9:58

Figure 4-5: *The New York Times,* like most publications, offers a two-week free trial.

If you have a Barnes & Noble gift card, you can add its value to your account. The gift card is used before your credit card is charged. See Figure 4-6. Here's how to associate a gift card with your account:

1. **Press the ∩ button to display the quick nav bar.**

2. **Tap the Settings button.**

3. **In the App Settings section, tap Shop.**

4. **Tap Gift Cards.**

5. Tap Add Gift Card.

6. Type the identifying number for the gift card (or other credit).

7. Type the PIN from the card.

You can register three gift cards, eGift cards, and online gift certificates at any one time. If you have more than that in your wallet, enter them after you've spent the others. When in doubt, call Barnes & Noble customer service for help.

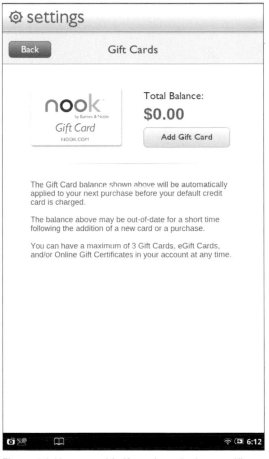

Figure 4-6: You can add gift cards and other certificates to your account, and purchases will be deducted from the current value.

Managing periodical subscriptions

You can cancel a subscription anytime and get credit based on the number of remaining issues in the billing period. Go to the magazine's offering page on www.BN.com to cancel the subscription.

If you buy an individual copy of a magazine or newspaper, you own it. It stays on your NOOK or in your B&N account for as long as you'd like. However, if you subscribe, the tablet only holds on to a specific number of issues.

The deletion of periodicals occurs automatically, whether you've read an issue or not. The oldest issue is deleted to make room for the newest. The number of issues your tablet keeps depends on how often issues come out.

That is, unless you archive your periodicals. (See this chapter's "Archiving and syncing your books.") When you archive a periodical, it's deleted from your tablet. You can always get it back, but you have to request it from deep storage.

Buying apps from B&N

The NOOK Tablet can accept new programs that teach it new tricks: apps. An *app* (short for application) is a small software program. Where do you get apps? Well, in the case of the NOOK Tablet, www.BN.com is the only official available source.

It remains to be seen how broad a range of apps the company will offer. At the launch of the NOOK Tablet, the app options were relatively insubstantial: no Skype, no online banking, no direct access to other reading material sources. There were some utilities that allow basic editing of Microsoft Office files, a few calendar and e-mail utilities, some cute games, and the first of what I expect will be a group of airline and travel apps. We can hope for more.

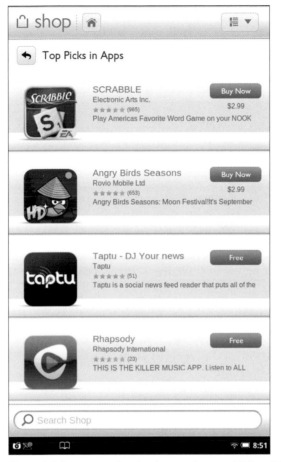

Figure 4-7: Apps extend and enhance the capabilities of the NOOK.

Here's how to buy an app:

1. **Press the ∩ button to display the quick nav bar.**
2. **Tap the Shop button.**
3. **In the Browse section, tap Apps.**

    Look at categories (Education & Reference, Games, Entertainment, Productivity, Tools & Utilities, Social, or News and Weather) or tap in the Search bar at the bottom of the screen and try to find what you're looking for.

Tap the name of an app to find out more details.

4. **Tap the green Buy Now button.**

You get to tap the Free button if it doesn't cost anything.

The file downloads to your tablet. If there's an interruption, the downloading starts back up when your WiFi is working properly. See Figure 4-8.

Figure 4-8: On the Daily Shelf, apps that are ready for download have a label saying just that.

You can shop for apps from your desktop or laptop computer, or from another device that can connect over the Internet to the B&N store (like a NOOKcolor eReader). Any purchases (or free apps) are included in your account; the next time you use your NOOK Tablet, you'll see the apps on the Daily Shelf with a Download badge. Tap the apps and they'll get to your tablet.

 A number of hackers succeeded in rooting the NOOKcolor. Expect the same with the NOOK Tablet. When a device is *rooted,* users can install apps that come from other sources (like Android Marketplace or directly from a programmer) and make other changes. The downside: B&N could update its operating system or refuse to honor warranty claims for a device that's been altered this way. (If you can use Erase & Deregister, that should remove all traces of rooting.) I'm not recommending you root your NOOK Tablet; in my opinion, if you feel you need a more capable tablet, it makes more sense to buy a different device.

Making a WishList

You can't always get what you want…but you can make lists about it. In fact, you can make multiple lists of wishes: one on your NOOK Tablet and one on www.BN.com. The most important difference between the two is that the NOOK Tablet's WishList is only for downloadable files. The website list can include paper books and other items you want to have shipped to you, as well as eBooks, magazines, and newspapers that can be downloaded to the NOOK Tablet. See Figure 4-9.

Adding to your WishList

To add a publication to your WishList:

1. **Go to** www.BN.com.

   You can visit from your NOOK Tablet, a desktop or laptop computer, or another web-capable device.

2. **Tap the cover to display details.**

3. **Tap the WishList check box.**

   The title is added.

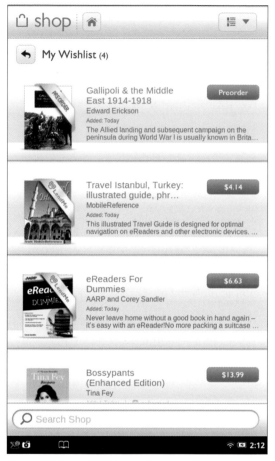

Figure 4-9: Your WishList can have media you want to buy later.

Checking your WishList

To view your WishList:

1. **Go to** www.BN.com.

2. **Tap the My Account button.**

3. **Tap the My WishList button.**

   A list shows the cover, title, and price of each item, along with the date each was added to your list.

4. **To buy something on your WishList, tap the price button next to the item.**

5. **Tap the Confirm button.**

Archiving and Syncing Your Books

Once you buy a book from Barnes & Noble, you own the license to that title on any device or application (up to the limit of six) registered to your account. You can leave the book file on your NOOK Tablet, or you can archive it back to your account, which removes it from the tablet but keeps it in your available material at www.BN.com.

You can also update, or sync, your NOOK Tablet to your BN.com account; doing so keeps it up to date with all of your currently purchased content — except for those you archived. Performing a sync lets you know about tablet updates, book loan offers, and other notices.

Performing a sync

Follow these steps:

1. **Make sure your NOOK Tablet's WiFi system is enabled and the device is successfully connected to the Internet.**

2. **Press the ∩ button to display the quick nav bar.**

3. **Tap the Library button.**

4. **Tap the Sync button.**

   It's in the lower-left corner and has an icon of two curved arrows forming a circle. The symbol reminds me of a dog who chased his own tail.

Archiving a publication

Follow these steps:

1. **Make sure your NOOK Tablet's WiFi system is enabled and the device is successfully connected to the Internet.**

2. **Press the ∩ button to display the quick nav bar.**

3. **Tap the Library button.**

4. **Press and hold on the book cover.**

   A menu offers several options.

5. **Tap Archive.**

   The book disappears from the Library, but it's on a shelf called Archived. See Figure 4-10.

Unarchiving a publication

Follow these steps:

1. **Make sure your NOOK Tablet's WiFi system is enabled and the device is successfully connected to the Internet.**

2. **Press the ∩ button to display the quick nav bar.**

3. **Tap the Library button.**

4. **Tap the My Shelves button.**

5. **Scroll through and find the Archived shelf.**

6. **Press and hold on the cover.**

   A menu appears.

7. **Tap Unarchive.**

   The book is removed from the Archived shelf and goes back to the Library.

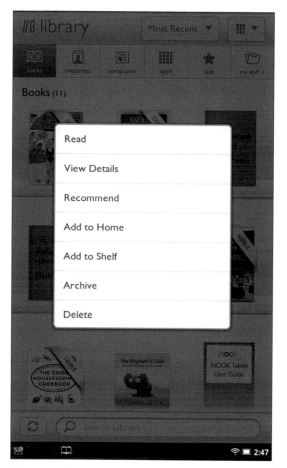

Figure 4-10: Archived books are removed from your desktop and Library, but you can get them.

Lending and Borrowing Books

The key to the LendMe program is the NOOK Friends network — people who are in your circle. You've invited them or they've invited you. Once they accept an invitation, you can lend and borrow books. See Figure 4-11.

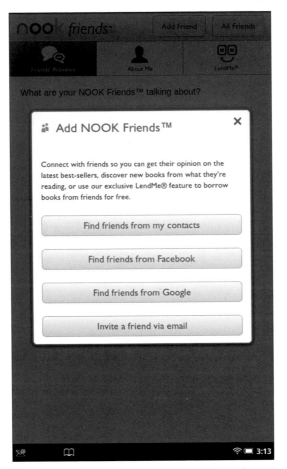

Figure 4-11: You can add NOOK Friends from various sources on your tablet.

You can invite friends from your Contacts list, from Facebook or Google, or by e-mail:

1. **Make sure your NOOK Tablet's WiFi system is enabled and the device is successfully connected to the Internet.**

2. **Press the ∩ button to display the quick nav bar.**

3. **Tap the Apps button.**

4. **Tap the Social Apps icon.**

Getting the tablet to its native area

What happens if you take your NOOK Tablet to an actual Barnes & Noble store (where there are walls and floors and ceilings)?

✔ The device asks if you'd like to connect to the InStore network. (Tap the Connect button to agree; tap the Dismiss button disagree.)

✔ If you do connect to the WiFi network at the store, you can get:

✔ A free pass to read or sample most NOOK eBooks for one hour per day free. You can read as many books as you want while you're in the store, although the 60-minute limit applies for each title.

✔ Exclusive content and offers available only to NOOK owners using the in-store network.

5. Tap NOOK Friends.

6. Tap the Add Friend button.

7. Choose a source of friends:

- Find Friends from My Contacts
- Find Friends from Facebook
- Find Friends from Google
- Invite a Friend Via Email

Lending a book

To lend a book from your Library, open the LendMe app. You can open it several ways:

✔ On the Home screen or the Daily Shelf, press and hold the book's cover. Tap LendMe in the menu that appears.

✔ In your Library, press and hold the book's cover. Tap LendMe in the menu that appears.

✔ In the book itself, tap the center of the page to display the reading tools. If a small blue flag appears at the right end of the slider, tap the blue flag. Tap the LendMe button.

A dialog box appears. From there, tap the icon that indicates how you want to notify someone of the LendMe offer:

- ✔ Send an e-mail by selecting one of your contacts. If you haven't entered any contacts or linked your account, select Contacts and press the Add Contact button.

- ✔ Post an offer on the person's Facebook wall. You must have previously linked your NOOK Tablet to your Facebook account.

- ✔ Send a notification by Google Gmail if you've linked your NOOK Tablet to that account.

Here are the conditions for the LendMe program from Barnes & Noble:

- ✔ While your book is loaned out, you can't read it on your own device.

- ✔ Not all books can be loaned. Look for a LendMe badge on a book cover.

- ✔ You can loan a book just once, and for no more than 14 days. A user can return the book any time during the loan. If it hasn't been returned at the end of 14 days, it's automatically returned.

- ✔ You can only loan one book at a time; you have to wait for a book to be returned before you can make another offer.

- ✔ You can only lend from a registered NOOK Tablet to users of other registered B&N devices, or applications that run on other devices such as desktop or laptop computers, smartphones, and certain other tablets.

- ✔ You can lend a book from anywhere with supported wireless connectivity (including WiFi hotspots outside of the U.S., U.S. territories, and Canada).

- ✔ You can send LendMe offers to any e-mail address, but to accept, the recipient must have an e-mail address associated with a Barnes & Noble online account, and that means a resident of the United States or Canada. An offer expires after seven days if it hasn't been accepted.

✔ You can't loan a book that has been loaned to you.

✔ You can't archive or save a borrowed book to the microSD card.

Another way to loan a book without restriction is to lend the actual NOOK Tablet device to a trusted friend or acquaintance. If you do this, be aware that the person will have access to the Barnes & Noble store under your account name (but can't buy anything if your account requires a password to do so).

Borrowing a book

You can also reach out and ask someone to lend you a book from their Library. To find out who has lendable books, launch the LendMe application. See Figure 4-12.

Here's how:

1. **Make sure your NOOK Tablet's WiFi system is enabled and the device is successfully connected to the Internet.**

2. **Press the ∩ button to display the quick nav bar.**

3. **Tap the Apps button.**

4. **Tap the Social button.**

5. **Tap NOOK Friends.**

   You'll see three shelves:

   • **My Lendable Books.** Books of yours that you can loan.

   • **Friends' Books to Borrow.** All the libraries combined of friends who have posted books for loan.

   • **Offers from Friends.** Specific offers from friends who are suggesting you borrow one of their titles.

6. **Tap the Borrow button next to the name of the book you want to read.**

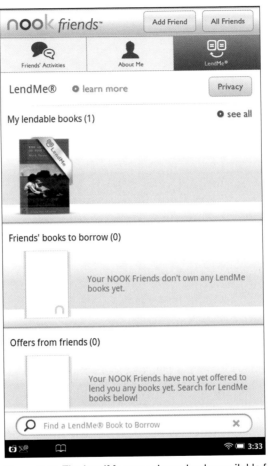

Figure 4-12: The LendMe page shows books available for loan or borrowing.

Setting Library privacy

Do you really want all of your friends to know the titles of all the books you have available for borrowing? Think it over: You may be disclosing some personal interests, political leanings, or other information you might want to keep to yourself.

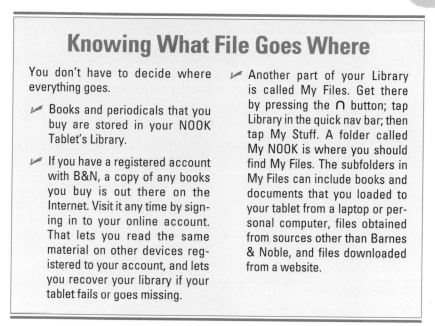

Knowing What File Goes Where

You don't have to decide where everything goes.

🖊 Books and periodicals that you buy are stored in your NOOK Tablet's Library.

🖊 If you have a registered account with B&N, a copy of any books you buy is out there on the Internet. Visit it any time by signing in to your online account. That lets you read the same material on other devices registered to your account, and lets you recover your library if your tablet fails or goes missing.

🖊 Another part of your Library is called My Files. Get there by pressing the ∩ button; tap Library in the quick nav bar; then tap My Stuff. A folder called My NOOK is where you should find My Files. The subfolders in My Files can include books and documents that you loaded to your tablet from a laptop or personal computer, files obtained from sources other than Barnes & Noble, and files downloaded from a website.

To decide what to keep to yourself, follow these steps:

1. **On the NOOK Friends page, tap the Privacy button.**

   The Privacy Settings page opens.

2. **Select (or deselect, if you want no books to show) the Show All of My Lendable Books to My NOOK Friends check box.**

   Or: Tap or drag a slider alongside the names of each of the lendable books in your Library. The switch toggles between Show and Hide.

The online library maintained in your name by Barnes & Noble keeps copies of all your purchases for a particular account, which lets you share titles across other devices (NOOKcolor, for example) or a NOOK application that runs on another device (including NOOK for PC, NOOK for BlackBerry, NOOK for iPhone, and NOOK for iPad). The key is that all devices or applications must be registered to the same account; as many as six devices are allowed.

Managing Your Library

The Library is where all documents live on your NOOK Tablet, including books, magazines, newspapers, and personal files. The Library is all inclusive, while the individual panels for Books, Magazines, and Newspapers hold only files that the system recognizes as fitting that description.

To some extent, you actually can tell a book by its cover on the NOOK Tablet: not so much about what's inside, but a great deal about its status or stature in your collection. See Figure 4-13.

Figure 4-13: Books and other publications can bear a badge that tells you more about their status.

✔ **New.** Freshly downloaded and ready to be opened. This badge goes away after the first time you open the document.

✔ **Sample.** A free sample of a book or other publication.

✔ **Download.** A publication that's either downloading or is waiting to be downloaded from www.BN.com.

✔ **Pre-order.** A title has been announced and is for sale, but isn't available for download yet. If you buy it, the book or publication will arrive at the first opportune moment.

✔ **Recommended.** A friend or contact has suggested that you check out this title.

✔ **LendMe.** A book that you can loan to someone.

✔ **Lent.** A book you are borrowing; the badge also indicates the number of days remaining on the loan. (While a book is loaned out, the original owner can't open it.)

Any search you start from your Library is done there only; if you start from the Home screen, the search expands, even looking at the B&N store if it can't find the title you want already on your tablet. To access the Search tool, tap the ∩ button to display the quick nav bar. Then tap the Search button.

Asking for a manual download

You might need to manually download content in certain situations, instead of relying on it to automatically appear. Here are some:

✔ You bought digital content and it wasn't automatically downloaded to your NOOK Tablet. This might have happened if your WiFi connection was terminated before the content was fully downloaded.

✔ You subscribed to a periodical but you (and your NOOK Tablet) have been out of WiFi reach.

✔ Your NOOK automatically deleted content because its internal memory was nearly full.

✔ You unregister and re-register your device to the same Barnes & Noble online account.

If an automatic or manual download fails (most often because of wireless connection problems), the NOOK Tablet will retry several times. If the download doesn't succeed, wait for a while and retry a manual download in an area where you have a strong WiFi signal.

The only way to connect to the Barnes & Noble website or elsewhere on the Internet from your NOOK Tablet is through a WiFi network. The NOOK Tablet eReader doesn't offer a cellular connection. And the supplied USB cable can transfer files from your computer; you can't connect through that computer to the Internet from the NOOK Tablet.

Building your own shelves

You can build your own shelves. Separate them as you see fit to organize your collection. When your NOOK arrives, it includes just one shelf: Favorites. But how about adding shelves to hold your vast collection of *For Dummies* eBooks, a few dozen of your favorite books by Corey Sandler, a special place for your cookbooks, and a separate group of emergency first aid guides in case something goes wrong in the kitchen but you are still able to read? See Figure 4-14.

Creating a shelf

You can create any shelf you want and call it anything you like. To create a shelf, do this:

1. **In My Library, tap My Stuff.**
2. **Tap Create a New Shelf.**
3. **Type a name for the shelf.**
4. **Tap Submit.**

Adding items to a shelf

Now you need to move things to your shelf. To add items:

1. **Highlight a book in the list of items in your Library.**
2. **Tap Shelves.**
3. **Tap Place On or Remove From Shelf.**

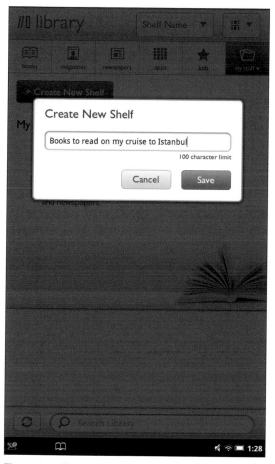

Figure 4-14: You can add custom shelves to hold particular groupings of publications.

4. **Tap a shelf.**

You can rename a previously created shelf by tapping Rename a Shelf on the touchscreen. To remove a shelf, tap Remove a Shelf; tap OK to confirm.

In some rare cases you may need to unlock a book or periodical that you bought through Barnes & Noble and that's protected using Digital Rights Management (DRM). In that case just enter your name, the e-mail address associated with the B&N account, and the credit card number that you used to make the purchase.

Going Elsewhere to Buy or Borrow

You can buy books from other sellers and download them to your NOOK Tablet. Many public libraries and educational institutions allow you to borrow reading material. Most of the files are in EPUB or PDF format, and they usually have Digital Rights Management (DRM) restrictions (to put a time limit on the loan of materials).

Lots of companies manage eBook loans with lots of tools. The leaders include Adobe Digital Editions and Overdrive. In addition, Amazon introduced in late 2011 a lending library for who bought their newer eReaders; that company, as is its wont, manages the lending process with its own Kindle tools. Other vendors of books, like Kobo, have their own systems.

About Adobe Digital Editions

The Adobe Digital Editions software is free and easy to use. See Figure 4-15.

Preparing to use NOOK Tablet with Adobe Digital Editions

Follow these steps to get ready:

1. **On a desktop or laptop computer, use a web browser connected to the Internet and go to** www.adobe. com/products/digitaleditions.

2. **Download the Adobe Digital Editions program.**

   Make sure it's the right version for your computer.

3. **Install the program on your desktop or laptop computer.**

4. **Follow the instructions to authorize your computer.**

5. **Turn on your NOOK Tablet.**

6. **Plug in both ends of the USB cable that came with your NOOK Tablet.**

   One end goes into the computer and the other end goes into the NOOK Tablet. Make sure to use the right USB cord.

   Adobe "recognizes" the tablet.

Installing book files using Adobe Digital Editions

When you've put Adobe Digital Editions on your laptop or desktop computer, you can use it to buy or borrow books from stores or libraries that require it. Follow the store's or library's instructions to download files to your computer. Then do the following:

1. **Launch Adobe Digital Editions on your desktop or laptop computer.**

2. **Turn on your NOOK Tablet.**

3. **Plug in both ends of the USB cable that came with your NOOK Tablet.**

   One end into the computer and the other into the NOOK Tablet. Make sure you don't force things!

4. **Drag files you have downloaded from their location on your computer's desktop or a folder onto the ADE library bookshelf.**

   They will be available for reading on the computer, but your goal is to get them onto your NOOK Tablet.

5. **Follow the instructions to move those files to an authorized NOOK Tablet.**

Diving into Overdrive

Some stores and libraries use a program called Overdrive. In one version it works a lot like Adobe Digital Editions. A second version goes directly on tablet computers.

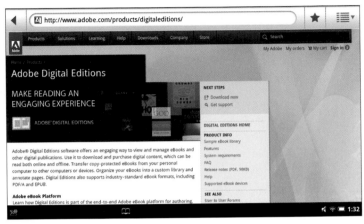

Figure 4-15: Adobe Digital Editions is downloaded to a desktop or laptop computer and used to authorize and then side-load files to your NOOK.

That said, as this book is being published, Overdrive isn't yet available for the NOOK Tablet. If and when it is, look for an app that you can install on your device. And then it will work like this:

1. **Download and install the Overdrive app on your NOOK Tablet.**

2. **Start Overdrive.**

3. **With your NOOK Tablet, go to a store or library where you have an account.**

4. **Choose and download book files to your device.**

If you're borrowing from a library, the book may come with a time limit. If you're buying from a store, the cost is charged to the account associated with the Overdrive app.

Overdrive is available for many Android-based tablets, but the NOOK Tablet is not amongst them, at least right now. Keep on the lookout, though.

Using Google ebookstore

You can buy a book at the Google ebookstore and start reading it on a NOOK Tablet. Maybe you want to continue reading the same book on your iPhone as you commute to work, read some more on the computer at your desk (during lunch hour, of course), and go out to dinner with a Sony eReader. As with the NOOK store, the books are tied to your account — not to a specific piece or brand. See Figure 4-16.

Figure 4-16: The Google ebookstore can provide current and classic literature.

Reading a public domain book via Google ebookstore

To read a public domain book, follow these steps:

1. **Go to** `http://books.google.com/ebooks`.

2. **Choose the book.**

3. **Save it to your personal computer.**

4. **Connect your NOOK Tablet to the computer using the USB cable.**

   Careful there. Make sure the cable came with your NOOK Tablet and make sure the right end goes into the right device.

5. **Load the file from the computer to the tablet.**

   Read how to side-load in Chapter 3.

6. **Install the latest version of Adobe Digital Editions on your laptop or personal computer.**

   If you haven't already, I explain how to do that earlier in this chapter.

7. **Enter an Adobe ID if prompted.**

   If you don't have an Adobe ID, you'll see a link onscreen to get one. From that point, anytime you buy an item online with a service (like Google ebookstore) that requires Adobe Digital Editions, the item is automatically associated with your Adobe ID, rather than your computer.

Buying on Google ebookstore

And now, here's how to buy a book on Google and move it to your NOOK Tablet:

1. **Go to** `http://books.google.com/ebooks`.

2. **Open a free account with Google.**

   The same account tags along if you use other Google tools, including Gmail.

3. **Select a book.**

4. **Click Buy.**

5. **Pay for the license to own a copy of the book.**

   The file is added to your Google account.

6. **In the list, find the book you want to transfer to the NOOK Tablet.**

7. **Click the About This Book button.**

8. **Click Read On Your Device.**

   You may see an EPUB version, a PDF version, or both.

9. **Click one of the links to transfer the ACSM file onto your computer.**

Be sure you know where the file is stored. You need the file to unlock the book. If you're given a choice between an EPUB or a PDF file format for an electronic book, go with EPUB: It is more likely to include most or all current features for the NOOK Tablet, like reflowable type, adjustments to typefaces, and more.

10. **Find the ACSM file on your computer.**

   It may be in a Downloads folder or on the desktop. If you can't find the file, search for ***.acsm**.

11. **Click the ACSM file.**

   The document should open in Adobe Digital Editions. If clicking the file doesn't open the Adobe software, find ADE on your computer (in My Programs) and start the program. Then select Add Item to Library from the Library menu, and find the ACSM file on your computer.

12. **If you aren't in Library view, click the icon in the top-left corner.**

   The book you bought from Google ebookstore doesn't show up in the All Items bookshelf in the Library view.

13. **Turn on your NOOK Tablet.**

14. **Connect your NOOK Tablet to the computer with the provided USB cable.**

   Adobe Digital Editions should recognize your NOOK Tablet as an authorized device and display it on the left pane of the software. If you don't see your NOOK Tablet, close Adobe Digital Editions and then reopen it with the USB cable in place, connected to your NOOK Tablet, which should be on.

15. **Click and drag the Google eBook in the right pane onto the NOOK Tablet icon in the left pane.**

   If you can't drag a book from the library to the NOOK Tablet, the Adobe software hasn't recognized your tablet as an authorized device. Consult the Adobe help screens.

   If you want to confirm the transfer, click the NOOK icon and find the book file there.

16. **Eject the NOOK Tablet from your laptop or personal computer before unplugging it.**

    Windows users can go to Explorer to find the NOOK and its memory card; right-click each and choose Eject. Macintosh users will find similar icons for the tablet in the Finder.

Getting something for nothing

Here are some worthy sites to visit for great free reads from authors who no longer need the money:

- ✓ **Project Gutenberg at** www.Gutenberg.org. Some of the files are plain text that you have to format and change to use. See Figure 4-17.

- ✓ **Manybooks.net at** www.Manybooks.net. Some of the same books you'll find on Project Gutenberg along with some new work by current authors.

- ✓ **Feedbooks at** www.Feedbooks.com. Plenty of 19th-century classics.

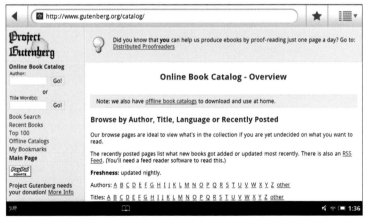

Figure 4-17: Project Gutenberg is a worldwide cooperative aimed at digitizing older, out-of-copyright books and publications.

Loading the right calibre

TIP

calibre is a free program you can download and install on your personal computer (Windows, Macintosh, or Linux). It converts files into EPUB or PDF format. With it you can also convert a PDF to a more flexible EPUB file. Get a copy of calibre at `http://calibre-ebook.com`.

Chapter 5

Going Wireless and Out on the Web

*I*f you have a WiFi system in your home or office, you should be able to connect to it and use your NOOK Tablet and pay nothing extra (beyond what you're already paying). When you travel, though, you may have to pay for time somewhere. All NOOK Tablet owners can use their device for free at a Barnes & Noble store.

 Your NOOK Tablet works perfectly well as an eReader and for many of its apps without a connection to a WiFi network. Here's what WiFi lets you do: browse the web, visit the online stores, and use e-mail.

Working Without a Wire

The Wireless Settings screen lets you turn WiFi on or off and it lists all the wireless networks your NOOK Tablet can find. The system asks if you want it to reconnect to any other network you have already used. The list of WiFi networks includes the name assigned by its owner and how strong the signal is (a stack of curved lines). The more dark lines you see, the better the signal. See Figure 5-1.

✔ To connect to an open or unsecured network, tap the network's name.

✔ To connect to a *secured network* (one that requires a password), tap the network name and then tap in the Password box. Type the required password (sometimes called a *key*) and tap Connect.

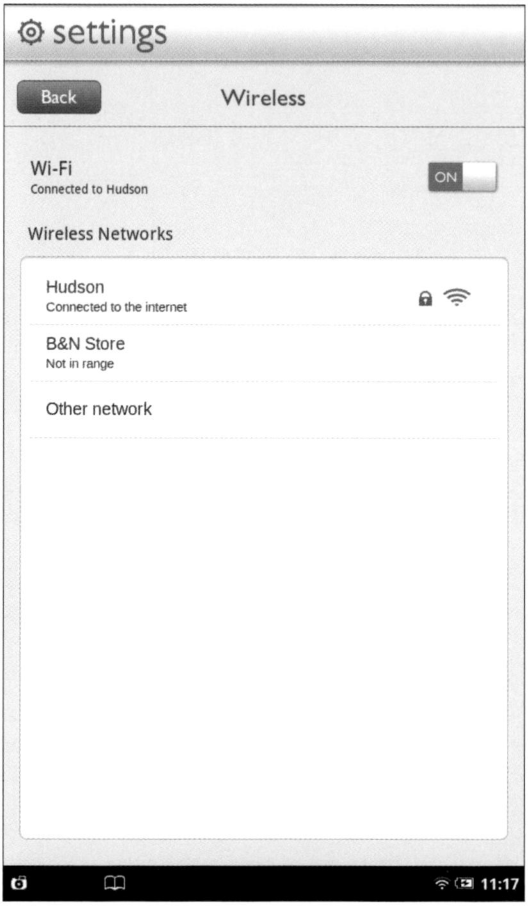

⚙ settings

Back		Wireless

Wi-Fi
Connected to Hudson
[ON]

Wireless Networks

Hudson
Connected to the internet   🔒 📶

B&N Store
Not in range

Other network

📶 📧 11:17

Figure 5-1: The Wireless Settings screen is the gateway to WiFi systems.

Some free networks offered at retail establishments give you the login information when you buy a drink or other item (not truly free, then, eh?); some hotels offer free service to registered guests. When you use this service, you may see all or none of the following:

- ✔ Terms and conditions
- ✔ A login screen
- ✔ Credit card information page (or other payment)

The NOOK Tablet will detect this sort of network, but you have to open a web browser window to enter the required details.

Using the web browser

The NOOK Tablet lets you visit web sites. The tablet's web browser is relatively fast and can show movies, news, and music. (For those who need to know: It supports Adobe Flash Player.)

To access the web browser, follow these steps:

1. **Make sure your NOOK Tablet is connected to a WiFi network.**
2. **Sign in if necessary.**
3. **Press the ∩ button to display the quick nav bar.**
4. **Tap the Web button.**

If the Web button on the quick nav bar looks gray and says Disabled, that means you can't choose it. You'll have to visit the Wireless Settings panel to fix that.

The NOOK Tablet's web browser should be familiar to anyone who has used a browser to cruise the web on a personal computer. Just like you can on a laptop, for example, you can open additional windows to quickly move from one page to another.

To open a new browser window, tap Options and then tap New Window. See Figure 5-2.

Options menu

Back button   Address bar   Favorites

http://www.sandlerbooks.com/Photos_by_Corey_Sandler.html

Figure 5-2: The NOOK web browser has most of the features that computer users expect.

The features are pointed out in Figure 5-2:

- **Address bar.** To visit a different page, tap in the address bar. Type an address and tap Go.

- **Back button.** To the left of the address bar, tapping the left arrow takes you to the page you most recently visited.

- **Favorites.** To the right of the address bar, tapping the star opens a window where you can mark favorite sites. You can view and edit the places you've visited *(browsing history)* and organize your favorites. Tap the thumbnail for the page you want to visit.

    On some computer browsers, favorites are called *bookmarks*. However, because the NOOK Tablet has an eReader, here they're called *favorites*. Same difference.

- **Options menu.** At the far right of the address bar, the down arrow opens a menu that lets you open a new window, open the Favorites list, and refresh the screen.

Marking your favorite spots

You can create a favorite (also known as a *web bookmark*) two ways. See Figure 5-3.

Adding a bookmark

To note the current web page as a favorite, do this:

1. **Press and hold anywhere on the page.**

   Do it anywhere except sections that are active (such as links or fields on a form). A good choice is usually a blank piece of the screen.

2. **From the menu that appears, tap Bookmark This Page.**

   A dialog box opens. And yes, I know it says Bookmark (at least in the first release of the software). It's a Bookmark/Favorite.

3. **Enter a name for the bookmark.**

4. **Accept the web address (URL) for the current location.**

   Or you can edit the name via the keyboard.

5. **Tap in the Name field.**

6. **Type something that identifies the bookmark.**

7. **Tap OK.** See Figure 5-3.

To create a favorite or a bookmark of the current page from the Options menu, do this:

1. **Tap the Options menu.**

2. **Tap the Bookmarks option.**

   The browser shows three tabs: Bookmarks, Most visited, and History. The Bookmarks tab is set to automatically open, and you will see rows of bookmarked web pages.

3. **Tap the Add+ thumbnail in the upper left of the window.**

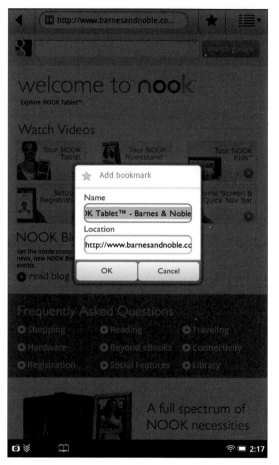

Figure 5-3: Bookmarks allow you to quickly jump to a favorite page on the web.

Deleting a favorite

Delete a web page bookmark this way:

1. **Tap the Options menu.**

2. **Tap the Bookmarks option.**

3. **Press and hold the thumbnail for the bookmark you want to delete.**

   A pop-up menu appears.

4. Tap Delete Bookmark.

5. Tap OK.

Adjusting the web browser's hair

The NOOK Tablet browser offers up five text sizes for web site text. Keep in mind that choosing a larger text size will make it easier to read but means you'll have to move around to see all the information on a page. See Figure 5-4.

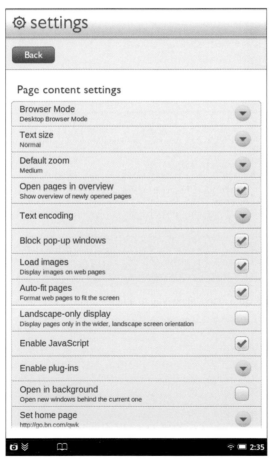

Figure 5-4: Page settings let you customize the web browser.

To change the text size, follow these steps:

1. **Tap the Options menu.**
2. **Tap More Options.**
3. **Tap Settings.**
4. **Tap Text Size.**
5. **Tap the text size you want to see in the browser.**

   Your choices are nicely named: Tiny, Small, Normal, Large, and Huge.
6. **Tap OK.**

   You can zoom in and out on an entire web page. On some pages that makes more sense than enlarging the text type.

To zoom in on a web page, quickly tap two times on the part you want to enlarge. Zoom out by tapping twice. After you zoom in, you can swipe left, right, up, or down to move around on the page. When you start moving around, plus (+) and minus (–) icons appear in the lower-left corner. Tap the (+) to zoom in more. Tap the (–) to zoom out.

Setting your home page

When you first use your NOOK Tablet's web browser, the home page is the Barnes & Noble store, which is devoted to all things NOOK. You're almost certainly going to want to return to there at some time, but speaking for myself I don't need to be assaulted by advertising every time, all the time. I suggest making it a bookmark for easy access.

Consider changing your home page to something that makes broader use of the wonders of the web. I prefer my daily web-based newspaper as my home page, or sometimes my personal website of photos. You can choose your own.

To change your home page:

1. **Tap the Options menu.**

   It's at the far right of the address bar; refer back to Figure 5-2.

2. **Tap More Options.**

   The Options menu closes and another menu opens.

3. **Tap the Settings option.**

4. **On the Settings screen, tap Set Home Page.**

   A dialog box opens.

5. **Type the web address (URL) for the page you want as your home page.**

6. **Click OK.**

Configuring web privacy and security

There are people out there who know if you've been sleeping and know when you're awake. What's more, they know if you've been bad or good. For goodness' sake — or at least for your own confidentiality — pay attention to your web browser's privacy settings. See Figure 5-5.

The NOOK Tablet doesn't have a bunch of security tools for Internet use. A clever Internet pirate may be able to get some of your personal information. Thieves are more attracted to laptop computers, but I recommend being picky about the information you store on your NOOK Tablet, and about any information you type into the Internet.

   ✔ Your first line of defense: **Use tough passwords** on any accounts you visit (like www.BN.com), and change the passwords from time to time.

   ✔ Your second line of defense: **Pay attention to privacy settings** on the NOOK Tablet and clear out personal information (like cookies) on a regular basis.

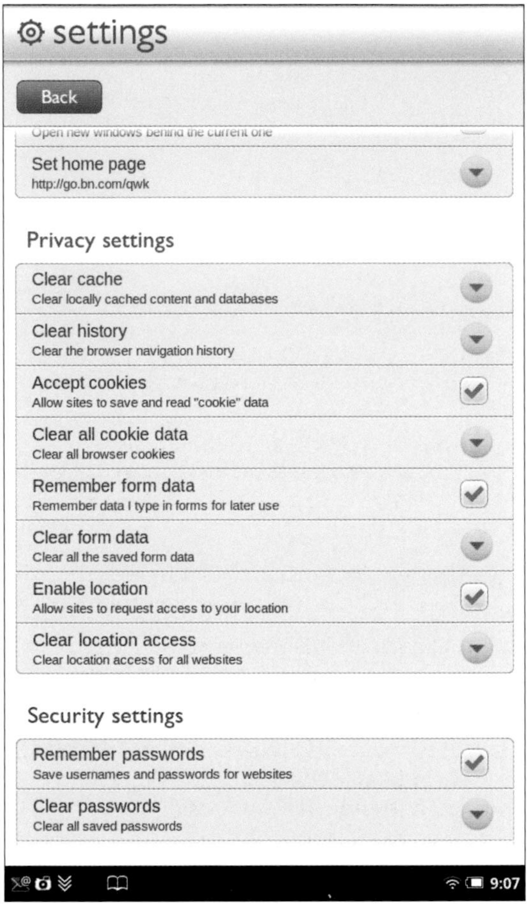

⚙ settings

[Back]

Open new windows behind the current one

Set home page
http://go.bn.com/qwk ▼

Privacy settings

Clear cache
Clear locally cached content and databases ▼

Clear history
Clear the browser navigation history ▼

Accept cookies
Allow sites to save and read "cookie" data ☑

Clear all cookie data
Clear all browser cookies ▼

Remember form data
Remember data I type in forms for later use ☑

Clear form data
Clear all the saved form data ▼

Enable location
Allow sites to request access to your location ☑

Clear location access
Clear location access for all websites ▼

Security settings

Remember passwords
Save usernames and passwords for websites ☑

Clear passwords
Clear all saved passwords ▼

✕@📷 ⨠ 🕮   ⤟ ▣ 9:07

Figure 5-5: Privacy settings let you clear web pages, cookies, and history stored on a NOOK Tablet.

To get to *either* web privacy or security settings, follow along:

1. **Start the web browser.**

2. **Tap the Options menu.**

   The Options menu is in the top-right of the address bar; refer back to Figure 5-2. When you click the arrow, a menu opens.

3. **Tap More Options.**

4. **Tap Settings.**

5. **Go to Privacy settings or Web Security settings.**

   With your finger, drag the screen up, past Page Content settings.

6. **Choose among options.**

   The options for web privacy and security settings are listed in the following sections.

Web privacy options

You can get to web privacy settings from the web browser's Options menu. Again, choose wisely (and conservatively):

✔ **Clear Cache.** If you tell the NOOK to clear the cache (pronounced *cash*), it will erase information about sites you have visited. To clear the cache, tap the down arrow and then tap OK.

✔ **Clear History.** To remove a list of recently visited web pages, tap on the down arrow and then tap on OK.

✔ **Accept Cookies.** This is turned on by default. To turn off this feature, clear the checkmark. (Note that some websites may not respond properly if you turn off cookies.)

   Some websites send a marker, a *cookie,* back to your tablet to indicate that you have visited the site, and sometimes to indicate choices or specific pages on the site you've explored.

✔ **Clear All Cookies.** To delete cookies, tap the down arrow and then tap OK.

✔ **Remember Form Data.** Your tablet can store data you've already typed into forms: things like your name, address, and phone number. This is turned on by default. To turn off this feature, clear the checkmark.

✔ **Clear Form Data.** To clear any stored form data, tap the down arrow and then tap OK.

✔ **Enable Location.** This allows sites to determine your general location by figuring out the location of the WiFi router you are using. To block this, clear the checkmark.

✔ **Clear Location Access.** Tap the down arrow and then tap OK to remove information about your location.

Web security options

You can get to web security settings from the browser's Options menu. Choose wisely.

- ✔ **Remember Passwords.** If you tap to place a checkmark in the box, the browser will ask you if you want to store usernames and passwords for websites. (Not all sites let you do this.)

- ✔ **Clear Passwords.** Tap the down arrow and then tap OK to clear all saved usernames and passwords.

- ✔ **Show Security Warnings.** Tap to place a checkmark in the box to be warned if there's a possible problem with a site's security certificate.

In most cases, warnings about security certificates aren't cause for concern. However, if you have any doubts, accept the warning as real and close the browser.

Adjusting web page content settings

The NOOK Tablet's browser has some features that not even the most advanced and costly tablets offer — among them, full-screen pages rather than the small versions aimed at smartphones.

To get to the web security settings:

1. **Start the web browser.**

2. **Tap the Options menu.**

   The Options menu is in the top right of the address bar; refer back to Figure 5-2. When you tap the Options arrow, a menu opens.

3. **Tap More Options.**

4. **Tap Settings.**

5. **In the Page Content settings section (at the top), choose an option:**

   - **Browser Mode.** Tap the down arrow and select between Tablet Browser Mode and Desktop Browser Mode, which will give you full websites.

- **Text Size.** Tap the down arrow to choose a standard text size. Your choices are Tiny, Small, Normal, Large, or Huge.

- **Default Zoom.** Tap the down arrow to adjust how the tablet reacts to a double-tap for a zoom-in. Choices are Far, Medium, or Close.

- **Block Pop-Up Windows.** The browser automatically blocks pop-ups (boxes that unexpectedly appear, and mostly to your annoyance). However, you may need or want to see them. You can block on or off from the Page Content settings of the web configuration options.

- **Load Images.** Uncheck the box to load web pages with placeholders — not actual images. This makes most pages come up faster. You can tap the markers to show individual images.

- **Auto-Fit Pages.** This nice option arranges web pages to fit the shape of your tablet automatically.

- **Enable JavaScript.** Many websites use JavaScript to display animation or special effects. You'll probably want to keep this on, although you might try shutting it off if you encounter problems with certain pages.

- **Set Home Page.** The NOOK Tablet has the Barnes & Noble welcome page as its home (starting page) anytime you open the web browser. To change the home page, tap the down arrow. Either tap the Use Current Page button or type a web address in the address bar.

Disabling and re-enabling the browser

Some users worry about leaving the door to the World Wide Web open all the time to all users. That might include parents who want to let the kids borrow the NOOK Tablet.

If you disable the browser, the tablet will still go to the B&N Store, although you can make sure someone has to enter a password to buy anything. However, you *won't* be able to do any of the following things:

✔ Surf the Internet

✔ Search the web from the quick nav bar

✔ Watch tutorial videos

✔ Use the Look Up feature (in the reading tools) for research in Google or Wikipedia

To disable the web browser, the first step is to set up a restrictions passcode that protects the browser setting. (Otherwise someone could just re-enable your NOOK Tablet's browser, despite your intentions.) Here are the steps:

1. **Press the ∩ button to display the quick nav bar.**

2. **Tap Settings.**

3. **Tap the Security option.**

4. **Tap Restrictions.**

5. **Tap the Restrictions check box.**

6. **Enter a four-digit code.**

   This passcode is different from the one you may have set as a device lock.

7. **Type the same code again when you're asked.**

8. **Tap the Restrict the Browser check box so that it's checked.**

   You can also put a mark in the Social Apps check box.

When the browser is disabled, the Web button in the quick nav bar will be grayed out and labeled Disabled.

To re-enable the web browser, follow these steps:

1. **Press the ∩ button to display the quick nav bar.**

2. **Tap Settings.**

3. **Tap the Security option.**

4. **Tap Restrictions.**

5. **Tap the Restrictions check box.**

6. **Enter the four-digit code for Restrictions.**

7. **Tap the Browser check box so that it's unchecked.**

Sending and Receiving E-mail

The NOOK Tablet comes with e-mail that lets you send and receive from most other e-mail programs: an account you have set up on your own or a web-based e-mail service like Gmail. See Figure 5-6. A few important notes:

✔ Your tablet must be connected to a WiFi network to receive and send e-mail.

✔ Barnes & Noble doesn't provide e-mail accounts.

✔ You can see the 25 most recent messages for each account (that you've linked to the NOOK Tablet, anyway).

Using the E-mail app

These steps assume you've set up an e-mail account with a provider (like Google for Gmail or your ISP). To launch and use the Email app, do this:

1. **Press the ∩ button to display the quick nav bar.**

2. **Tap Apps.**

3. **In the Apps window, tap Email and choose the automatic setup.**

   You're taken to the Inbox. If you haven't visited the Email app yet, you're taken to a screen so you can set it up.

4. **Type the address for your e-mail account.**

5. **Enter the password for the account.**

6. **(Optional) Tap the check box for Send E-mail from This Account by Default.**

7. **Tap Next.**

   The NOOK Tablet tries to connect. This will usually succeed if you're using one of the common web-based services like Gmail, Hotmail, or Yahoo! Mail. You're notified if all goes well; if not, you will see an error message. If you get an error message, try setting up manually. Those instructions are in the next section of this chapter.

8. **(Optional) Type a name for this account.**

A name can help you distinguish among multiple accounts. If you don't want to name the account, leave the option blank.

9. **Enter your name as you want it to appear in e-mail messages that you send.**

Recipients see this name in the From field on their Email app.

10. **Click Done.**

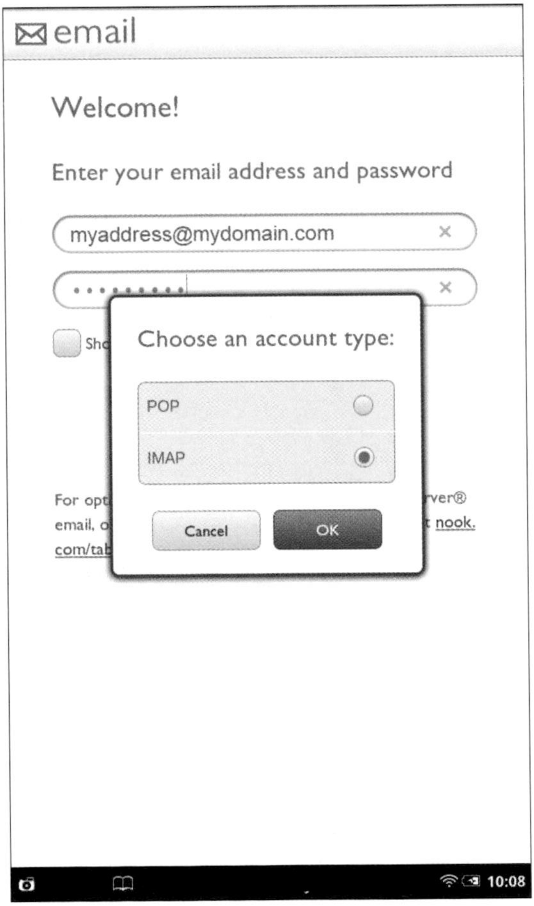

Figure 5-6: Choosing an e-mail protocol is an essential element of configuring an account.

Setting up an account manually

If automatic setup doesn't work, set up your Email app account manually. **You have to know the exact name of your provider's e-mail server for sending and receiving.** You should be able to find that by consulting help or FAQ pages for the provider, by calling their help desk (some are more helpful than others), or by examining the Properties setting on an existing e-mail program on your desktop or laptop computer. See Figure 5-7.

To set up an e-mail account manually, follow these steps:

1. **Press the ∩ button to display the quick nav bar.**

2. **Tap Apps.**

3. **In the Apps window, tap Email.**

   You're taken to the Inbox. If you haven't visited the Email app yet, you're taken to a screen so you can set it up. You have to choose between automatic and manual configuration. Both ways are described next.

4. **Type the address for your e-mail account.**

5. **Enter the password for the account.**

6. **(Optional) Tap the check box for Send E-mail from This Account by Default.**

7. **Tap Manual Setup.**

   The Server Settings screen opens.

8. **Choose an account type: POP or IMAP.**

9. **Tap OK.**

10. **Enter the name of the POP or IMAP server.**

    For example, it might be something like IMAP.*isp_ server.com*.

    Some systems have extra security requirements or use a non-standard port (the gateway from your tablet to the Internet). Unless your provider has told you otherwise, leave these settings unchanged.

11. **Tap Next.**

    If the NOOK Tablet connects with the e-mail provider, it shows you another setup screen.

Figure 5-7: Get your server name and other specific information from your e-mail provider.

12. **Enter the name of the SMTP server.**

An example might be something like SMTP.*isp_server.com*.

If all goes well, you see one final page.

13. **Make a time selection.**

This is how often the tablet will check for new e-mail.

14. **Indicate whether you want to hear a chime when you get new e-mail.**

15. **Tap Next.**

16. **Tap Done.**

Sending an e-mail

Sending a message is very simple.

1. **Tap the pencil icon in the upper-left corner.**

   The icon is pointed out in Figure 5-8.

2. **Type an address in the To box.**

   Or you can tap the Contacts icon and choose an address. Separate additional names with a comma.

   If you've set up more than one e-mail account, you can switch by tapping Account (at the top of the Email screen). Choose the inbox for the account you want to check. You can also select Combined Inbox to see all messages from all established accounts in a single listing.

3. **Type a message.**

4. **Tap Send.**

Your NOOKy Hancock

When you send a message from your NOOK Tablet's Email app, this is tagged on at the bottom of every one: "Sent from my NOOK." If you'd rather not send advertising, change your signature:

1. Open the NOOK Email app.

2. Tap the down arrow.

3. Select the Accounts option.

4. Tap the gear icon next to the account you want to configure.

5. In the General tab, tap the Signature line's down arrow there.

6. Edit or delete the text you find in the Signature block.

7. Tap OK.

Replying to or forwarding a message

Forwarding a message sends a copy of the message to someone else. The process is nearly identical to that of Reply. Here's how:

1. **Open an e-mail message.**

2. **Tap Reply.**

   Some day you're going to thank me for this one: Be *very careful* before you choose Reply All if you intend to crack wise, complain, or pass along some comment you may someday regret. Choose Reply All only after you have duly considered all of the potential consequences and studied all of the addresses to which your response will be sent.

3. **Tap Forward.**

   The Compose screen opens.

4. **Type the e-mail addresses to send the message to.**

   You can add a note of your own, like "This is the funniest joke I've ever heard." The original subject line goes along with the message, along with Fwd:. You can edit the subject if you'd prefer. See Figure 5-8.

5. **Tap Send.**

Look carefully at a message before you send it. Do you really want *all* recipients to know *all* the information it has? Are you possibly violating someone's expectation of privacy by passing along *all* e-mail addresses? Remember, too, that a recipient of a forwarded message might choose to forward it to a new group of people, spreading its contents (and e-mail addresses) to people you don't know. I generally edit out all unnecessary information from messages I forward.

Start a new e-mail   Delete chosen messages

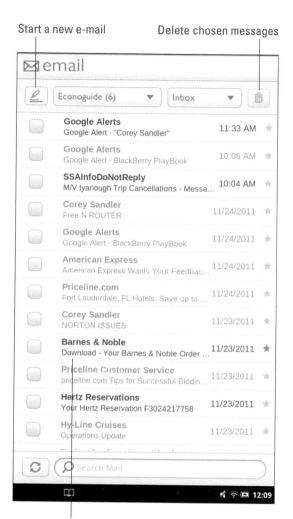

An unopened message

Figure 5-8: The NOOK Tablet e-mail panel shows unopened messages in bold.

Deleting e-mail

To get rid of a message you have open, tap the Delete button at the bottom of the screen.

If the message you want to get rid of isn't open, go to the Inbox and follow these steps:

1. **Tap the check box next to the message(s) you want to delete.**

2. **Tap the trash can icon at the upper-right corner of the screen.**

Getting attached

Can you remember your first attachment? The thrill of victory, the agony of defeat.

Enough about high school. Let's talk about our mature, modern lives. A time when we use our high-tech computer tablets to send photographs of the grandchildren, video clips of cats stuck in shoe boxes, and singing birthday cards. Most of those are sent as *attachments* to e-mails, which means you're sending a separate file along with the text of a message.

If you get a message with attachments, tap the View Attachments button.

The NOOK Tablet can work with PDF files or Microsoft Office word processing, spreadsheet, and simple PowerPoint files. The NOOK will store e-mail attachments in the MyFiles/Downloads folder. In the first release of the operating system for the NOOK Tablet, you can receive attachments but cannot send them. This oversight may be fixed in later updates.

Putting Your Social Affairs in Order

Your NOOK Tablet comes ready to work with some Facebook or Twitter features; you can import your contacts from a Google Gmail account. All of this, of course, requires that your

NOOK Tablet be connected to a WiFi network and signed in. See Figure 5-9.

🗸 On **Facebook** you can post recommendations, comments, quotations, and LendMe offers on your own wall or on a friend's who's given you that access. In Facebook lingo, you can "like" a book to declare your feelings. You can even tell the world of your "reading status" if you think it's important to declare that you've reached page 125.

🗸 Then there are the tweets that tumble to your tablet from **Twitter.** If you let your NOOK use your account, you can read Tweets, see the online names of the people you follow, follow someone new, and update your profile.

The Twitter exceptions: You can't get to your direct messages or set your Twitter password from the special app on the NOOK Tablet. However, you *can* go to the NOOK Tablet's web browser and sign into Twitter if you want to do those tasks.

🗸 The world of **Google** is burgeoning. When you link your account to the NOOK Tablet, you can move amongst most of the Google apps, including Gmail.

To link a NOOK Tablet to one of these social networking accounts:

1. **Press the ∩ button to display the quick nav bar.**

2. **Tap the Settings button.**

3. **In the Settings panel, scroll down to App Settings and tap Social.**

4. **Tap Manage Your Accounts.**

5. **Link your Facebook, Twitter, or Google accounts.**

   Each website has a different login screen, and their features will change over time: I guarantee you.

If you don't have an account with Facebook, Google, or Twitter, you can sign up through the page displayed on your NOOK Tablet. You may find, though, that it's easier to sign up, customize, and enhance your page from a personal computer. Wherever you connect to one of these services, all your actions are linked.

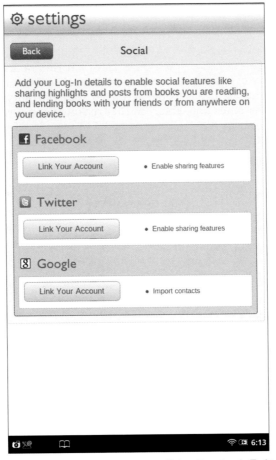

Figure 5-9: The NOOK Tablet can link to Facebook, Twitter, and Google.

App-lying Yourself

Your NOOK Tablet runs the Android operating system. That's a very good thing, because Android (developed by Google) has been adopted by a wide range of smartphones and tablets; because of that, lots of people have made *applications* (or *apps* — small programs) that can run on these devices.

At least officially, the only source of add-on programs for the NOOK Tablet is through the NOOK App Store.

Some users of the NOOKcolor eReader, which is the older and cousin to the NOOK Tablet, have *rooted* their device so they can have access to most of the Android device apps without having to go through the B&N Store. (Neither the NOOKcolor or the NOOK Tablet has a camera, which eliminates one large category of apps.) If you explore this route to rooting, be aware that Barnes & Noble may void your warranty if your tablet becomes unusable. For that reason, I'm not recommending you root; that said, you'll find abundant information about rooting a NOOK if you look on the web.

The supplied apps

The NOOK Tablet comes with some applications. Press the ∩ button to display the quick nav bar and then tap Apps. Here are the apps that came with the first release of the tablet:

- ✔ **Chess.** This well-designed version of the classic game lets you play against the computer at easy, normal, or hard levels. You can apply a clock to the game and select color schemes.

- ✔ **Contacts.** A manager for names, addresses, phone numbers, and e-mail addresses. Once you add a contact, you can use it in the Email app as well as the social network apps.

- ✔ **Crossword.** 56 Across: Lots of fun for logophiles. The clue appears when you choose a column or row. I especially like that the font looks like handwriting. The games are challenging, though not quite up to the level of *The New York Times*. See Figure 5-10.

- ✔ **Music Player.** With this program you can play music files that you've downloaded (or side loaded; see Chapter 3) to your NOOK. I discuss the player in the next section of this chapter.

- ✔ **My Media.** (Also called the Gallery in some references on the tablet and in the instruction manual.) This all-purpose picture collector and video player works with files you downloaded or side loaded to your NOOK. (Again, see Chapter 3 for side-loading instructions.)

- ✔ **NOOK Friends.** This is Barnes & Noble's own version of a social network combined with a lending library. You can communicate with those you have befriended, sharing recommendations and comments and lending books — subject to certain restrictions.

✔ **Sudoku.** The addictive — to some — Japanese number puzzle is here on your tablet. If this is what you're looking for, this is a fine example.

Figure 5-10: Crossword is a worthy complement to an educated reader.

This chapter already explores the Email app, part of the basic operating system. The NOOK Tablet also comes with three preinstalled links to streaming video and music services:

  ✓ Pandora

  ✓ Hulu Plus

  ✓ Netflix

I discuss those later in this chapter.

Music player

Audio sounds a little better if you plug a set of earbuds into the headphone output jack. (Figure 1-1 in Chapter 1 can help you find it.) See Figure 5-11. The NOOK plays most of the common file formats, including MIDI, MPEG, WAV, AAC, and AMR.

Moving audio files onto the NOOK Tablet

To transfer audio files onto the NOOK Tablet:

1. **Connect your NOOK Tablet to a personal computer using the microUSB cable.**

   Use the cable that came with the device or an identical cable; don't use a generic cable. (The cable detaches from the AC adapter; that end is a standard USB plug that you can attach to a desktop or laptop computer.)

   On your desktop or laptop computer, the NOOK Tablet shows up as a new disk drive called MyNOOK (or, on some devices, as a Removable Drive with a letter code). If a microSD(HC) memory card is in your NOOK Tablet, it will also show up in My Computer (Windows) or in the Finder (Macintosh).

2. **Drag the files onto the MyNOOK drive or the memory card.**

   Put audio files in the Music folder in My Files.

3. **Eject the media drive.**

   The official instructions say this is a must. Microsoft Windows usually has a Safely Remove Hardware icon in the system tray. Or go to My Computer, highlight and right-click the drive, and choose Eject.

4. Unplug the USB cable.

Drag to change song order

Click to choose Now Playing mode

Now playing

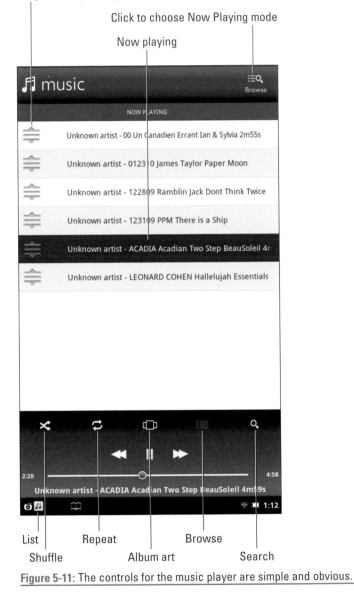

List

Shuffle

Repeat

Album art

Browse

Search

Figure 5-11: The controls for the music player are simple and obvious.

Playing an audio file from the Library

You can start the music player

- ✔ By tapping a music file
- ✔ By tapping the music player icon
- ✔ From the Library shown in Figure 5-12

Here's how to do the latterest:

1. **Press the ∩ button to display the quick nav bar.**
2. **Tap My Stuff.**
3. **Tap the My Files icon.**
4. **Find and tap the Music folder.**
5. **Tap the file you want to play.**

    The music starts up.

Launching the music player directly

To launch the music player application directly:

1. **Press the ∩ button to display the quick nav bar.**
2. **Tap the Apps icon.**
3. **Tap the music player icon.**

The music app has two modes: Browse and Now Playing. A red (not rock) band tells you which mode you're in. To switch modes, tap the icon in the upper-right corner of the screen. Tap three times on the ceiling if you're a Tony Orlando fan.

In Browse mode, you can choose from these options:

- ✔ **Shuffle.** (Icon: two crossed arrows) The tablet randomly selects and plays songs from your collection.
- ✔ **Repeat.** (Icon: two arrows in a loop) Tap once to repeat all your songs; tap tap twice to repeat the current track.
- ✔ **Album art.** (Icon: a box) See artwork for the track that's playing.

✔ **Browse.** (Icon: a stack of horizontal lines) See available tracks.

✔ **Search.** (Icon: a magnifying glass) Hunt through your NOOK Tablet files to find a particular song or artist.

✔ **List.** (Icon: musical note) See songs and times.

✔ **Artist.** (Icon: microphone) See songs by the artist's name.

Figure 5-12: Music files are considered media, like other items in the NOOK Library.

When you're using the music player in Now Playing mode, you can press and hold the gray arrow (to the left of a song title) and drag the file up or down in the list to change the song order.

Opening That Box: Pandora Radio

I am old enough to remember radio; in fact, I remember the days before they were portable; big boxy things with a plug. But Pandora has opened another box. See Figure 5-13. Think of it as your personal electronic disk jockey that starts with a few songs or artists you like and then finds music that's similar or shares certain attributes.

You get to create and fine-tune your own stations. You can have as many as 100 channels and play just one, or rotate through them all, or ask the tablet to play randomly. The basic Pandora Internet Radio service is free, but an enhanced, commercial-free subscription is sold for certain devices. As this book goes to press, the Pandora app on the NOOK Tablet only runs the free (with advertising) version; however, if you go to the web browser on the NOOK Tablet and visit www. pandora.com, you can use the full site for free or sign up for ad-less music for a reasonable annual fee.

 To use Pandora (and Hulu Plus, about which you read about shortly) you must have a membership; it's separate from your account with Barnes & Noble. If you have a previously established Pandora account, you can sign in to it from the NOOK Tablet; if not, you can set up one from the tablet or from a desktop or laptop computer.

 You must have an active WiFi connection to listen to Pandora; it can play in the background while you read or shop or use other elements of the NOOK Tablet. Use the Home button on the quick nav bar to move somewhere else. While Pandora plays, a small P icon appears on the right side of the status bar. Tap this icon to return to the Pandora app.

Figure 5-13: Pandora gives you a personal musical curator on the Internet.

Video Playing On

The NOOK Tablet's high-resolution, full-color screen is quite capable as miniature TV, although the screen size is obviously more suited for solo watching up close.

You can use this facility three ways:

✓ Visit websites that offer free video on demand. These include sites like www.youtube.com, computer and electronics review sites like www.cnet.com, and TV networks like www.nbc.com. For best results, choose a file intended for a tablet.

✓ Subscribe to services like Hulu Plus and Netflix. (I discuss these in the following sections.)

✓ Watch videos that you've side loaded. (See Chapter 3 for instructions.) The videos may be ones you took with your video camera or cellphone, or they may be works you got (legally). Transfer compatible video files from a personal computer using the USB cable; follow the same instructions you would for transferring music and audio files. Those instructions are in this chapter's "Moving audio files onto the NOOK Tablet" section.

The best quality videos are in MP4 and M4V file formats. The other acceptable file formats come from the small-screen world of smartphones, including 3GP. To play a video that you've loaded onto your NOOK Tablet, find and tap it. (One route: Tap the ∩ button; tap Library, and then tap My Stuff. Find the file in the Video or Downloads folder.) If you try to load and run a file that isn't supported, it simply won't play.

In most cases you can't enlarge a video that you're playing from a file that's stored on the NOOK Tablet; the pinch-out gesture may work with some streaming video websites, though.

Subscribing to Hulu Plus

Hulu Plus brings current and older TV shows, and some movies, to your tablet over the Internet on a monthly subscription basis. See Figure 5-14. Shows generally have limited advertising.

Figure 5-14: Catch up on certain TV shows and movies using Hulu Plus.

Hulu Plus and Netflix videos are *streamed* to your device and not stored on it. The only way to watch television shows or movies offered by these services is with an active WiFi connection to the Internet.

Your NOOK Tablet has an app that takes you directly to the Hulu Plus website; you can also get there by using the web browser and going to www.hulu.com/plus. You can sign up for the service from your NOOK Tablet or from a desktop or laptop computer. (The original free service, Hulu, isn't available on the NOOK Tablet.)

Subscribing to Netflix

Netflix is one of the main providers of streaming video (and they're streaming to everything from PCs to Internet-connected TVs, to handheld devices — including your NOOK Tablet. You can sign up for a monthly subscription.

Netflix shows only in landscape mode on the tablet, and offers thousands of movies. Not all the Netflix library is available to stream; some are offered only in DVD form. Visit www.netflix.com and explore some of the library.

Chapter 6

The Part of Tens-Plus: Tips and Tricks

A printed book is not high tech. It has no batteries, no microprocessor, no screen. You can fix most technical failures related to paper books with tape. But a piece of technology isn't likely to be fixed that way. Things happen. Conditions change. Settings can go awry. And not all of the problems are the fault of we humans. Even pieces of hardware can become confused and stutter to a stop. In this chapter I try to anticipate as many of the possible problems as I can imagine. Even better, I offer some suggestions for making things right, plus one or two tips and tricks you might not otherwise be aware of.

But wait, there's more: In this section I expound a bit on a certain number of not-so-obvious things you should know about the NOOK Tablet. There's no need to count. When we talk about a part of tens, that's only for those who think in classical digital form. (*Digital* as in a mathematical system based around units of ten, which made eminent sense tens of thousands of years ago when early humans finally realized that most of them were born with ten fingers and ten toes.)

Computer math is extensible and almost infinitely adjustable. There are binary systems (powers of two), decimal systems (tens), hexadecimal systems (a base of 16), and then there is the very special *NOOK Tablet For Dummies* "No Extra Charge Additional Tips Section."

Making a Screen Capture

You won't find it in the official NOOK Tablet user guide, but here's how to grab a *screen capture* (also called a *screenshot*): Press the ∩ button and the – volume button (on the right side of the device) at the same time. It may take a few tries to get the hang of it; if you've done it correctly, you'll hear a tone and see a tiny icon of a camera appear in the lower-left corner status bar.

Tapping that camera icon opens a notifications bar, where you can see confirmation that you captured a screenshot. See Figure 6-1. If you tap that notification, your NOOK Tablet will go to My Media and launch the image. And the image itself has been saved in the Screenshots folder, which you can get to from My Files.

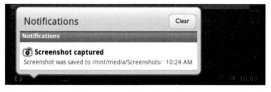

Figure 6-1: You'll see a notification that a screenshot has been captured; tap the message to go directly to the gallery to see it.

If you connect your tablet to a desktop or laptop computer using the USB cable, you can copy the files to your PC. And yes, that is exactly how I got the screen captures in this book.

Screenshots are saved as png files, which are *lossless* compressed files at the full screen resolution of 600 x 1024 pixels. In other words, the quality is quite good and the size is quite reasonable.

I said earlier that you can capture "most" screens. Some applications, including videos, may not let you. There is one other little gotcha you may need to keep in mind: When you make a screen capture, it's numbered this way: 11-11-22-1.png, meaning 2011, November 22 #1, and so on. If you copy those screen captures to your PC and clear the tablet, future screenshots will renumber back to 1, so at least on a single day you could end up with multiple files with the same name. Fix this problem by changing the filenames on your desktop or laptop computer.

Reawakening a Dead NOOK Tablet

Okay, not really a *dead* unit. That would be beyond my skills. But some things can make a NOOK Tablet appear dead even when it isn't ready for the recycle bin. The usual suspects look like the following.

Not enough battery power

The NOOK Tablet's rechargeable battery doesn't have an endless source of energy; you must recharge it. Depending on how you use your device (including whether you are online for an extended period of time), you may need to recharge the battery daily, or you may have to recharge it just once a week.

If your NOOK Tablet starts acting squirrely, check the battery level. Anytime the device is on the Home screen or in most text-based books, you will see a battery icon in the bottom-right corner. To see more precise information, go to Settings and then tap Device Info to see the percentage remaining.

Your recharger isn't getting juice

I'm pretty advanced when it comes to technical matters but I do have a confession to make: I once paid a washing machine repairman good money to learn that the machine wasn't performing properly because the water faucet was turned off. The same sort of situation can arise with a battery recharger. Make sure it's plugged into a live outlet; try to avoid using an outlet that is controlled by a wall switch. If the charger is attached to a power strip, make sure that device is on. You can test an outlet or strip by plugging a lamp into it.

The recharger design can also be mischievous. There is a charger, and a separate USB cable runs between the charger and the tablet. Make sure that the cable is properly and fully attached at each end and that the little ∩ icon at the reader end of the cable glows. It's orange while it charges and green when it's done charging.

Putting the Battery to the Test

Your NOOK Tablet's lithium ion battery should deliver a nice charge for several years. If the battery fails during the standard one-year warranty period, you'll have to send it in for repair. Get an idea of how juiced up your tablet is by going to the Quick Settings screen shown in Figure 6-2.

Modern high-capacity rechargeable batteries get warm as they're used. It's highly unlikely, but a faulty battery could be fire risk. If you believe the internal battery is generating too much heat or is otherwise acting oddly, turn the thing off and contact Barnes & Noble customer service at 1-800-843-2665.

Now, consider things you can do to make the battery last as long as possible:

- **Don't let the battery become fully run down.** Turn off the tablet when you see the low charge alert. Recharge the battery fully before you use it again.

- **Avoid extremely high or low temperatures.** Don't take your tablet to the ski lodge or on your sub-Saharan photo shoot.

- **Don't let your battery get scorching hot while the tablet's running.** If your tablet is so hot you could fry an egg on it as you read the morning newspaper, do these three things:

- Carefully unplug it.
- Turn off the power.
- Call B&N customer service at 1-800-843-2665.

🖌 **Recharge the battery before a prolonged period on the shelf.** If you plan to put your tablet away for more than a week, charge the battery until it's at least half full. Then turn it off completely by pressing and holding the power button for 3 seconds.

Figure 6-2: Quick Settings lets you check on your battery.

Barnes & Noble urges you to use only the AC adapter and the USB cable that came with your NOOK Tablet. If you need a second charger, they'll be happy to sell you one. (That's not to say that other manufacturers may not offer their own fully capable version of the charger; here in this section I'm just passing along the official word. If you choose to use a charger from another company, make certain it exactly matches the electrical specifications of the manufacturer's original device.)

Keeping a NOOK Tablet Happy

The NOOK is an electrical device. To keep it happy, keep it cool, dry, and all together in one piece.

- ✔ **Keep it dry.** Don't take the NOOK into the bathtub with you — or out into a thunderstorm or into the steam room. I also strongly suggest keeping cups and cans of caffeine far away. A little bit of water can wreck the tablet.

- ✔ **Keep it cool.** Never leave the NOOK in a closed car in the summer heat, and don't put it on a radiator in the winter.

- ✔ **Keep it in one piece.** Although the NOOK is reasonably sturdy, don't put it in your back pocket or use it to prop a rocking table.

Exits to the Right; Power Button to the Left

You're likely to be asked to turn off your NOOK Tablet in places like airplanes, hospitals, and laboratories. Follow the instructions of flight attendants, doctors, nurses, and anyone else who has a real reason to ask you to turn off your NOOK Tablet.

To turn off the NOOK Tablet's WiFi networking, tap the right end of the status bar to open the Quick Settings dialog box; then slide the Wireless switch to Off. Tap anywhere outside the Quick Settings dialog box to close it. Do the same, but choose On, to re-enable WiFi.

The biggest concern is the WiFi radio, although (just between you and me) I think this is a bogus issue. WiFi is just about everywhere now, including hospitals and airplanes. A slightly bigger concern would be cellular systems, although even that is probably not a real issue except on board an airplane; it's not a matter of interference with the plane's electronic systems but the fact that a cellphone trying to connect with cell towers on the ground could easily end up linking to dozens of antennas at the same time.

Caring for the Touchscreen

You should keep your touchscreen clean for three good reasons:

- It might stop responding to your touch if there is too much gloop on it.
- The image will look pretty bad if you have to view it through a layer of french fry grease.
- Do you really want people to see your handsome, high-tech NOOK Tablet covered with smudges, smears, and schmutz?

Try to keep your hands clean; don't go out and change the oil in your car and then swipe your fingers across the touchscreen. Clean up first. Also, consider buying a little home for your NOOK. A carrying case or sleeve can help protect and keep it clean.

Here's how to clean the touchscreen:

1. **Press and hold the power button for about 5 seconds to turn off the NOOK.**

2. **Wipe with a soft cloth.**

   I recommend using one of those specialized microfiber cloths made for cleaning eyeglasses.

- *Don't* use any chemicals to clean the screen. If necessary, you can make the cloth *slightly* damp.
- *Don't* run the screen (or the cloth) under the faucet.

Improving Your NOOK Tablet Warranty

Your NOOK comes with a warranty. Don't be shy about calling technical support or visiting a Barnes & Noble store and seeing their specialist for help.

The basic warranty from Barnes & Noble protects against unit failure. If the screen stops lighting up, the speakers buzz instead of sing, or if WiFi is no longer wide nor of good fidelity, the company promises to repair or replace it with an equivalent model (which may be new or may be a "remanufactured" model returned by a previous owner). This sort of warranty is standard.

It's important to understand what the warranty doesn't cover:

- ✔ Your NOOK Tablet tumbling to the floor.
- ✔ Your NOOK Tablet getting caught in a folding recliner.
- ✔ Your NOOK Tablet splashing into the bathtub.

You can, however, buy a bit of assurance (but not *in*surance). One is the B&N Protection Plan, which replaces or repairs your NOOK Tablet if there's *accidental* damage (of the sort I just wrote about) two years from the day you bought it; it also extends the warranty against defects.

- ✔ The plan costs about 25 percent of the original purchase price.
- ✔ The plan *doesn't* protect you against mishaps that aren't accidental. If you admit to taking the NOOK into the shower or confess to microwaving it for science class, they're not going to laugh along with you.
- ✔ The plan *doesn't* cover a lost or stolen NOOK Tablet. To protect against that, get in touch with your insurance agent to see if you're protected under your homeowner's or renter's policy; some automobile policies also cover items that are stolen from a car.

Premium-level credit cards from American Express, MasterCard, and Visa generally offer added protection for devices that you've bought with those pieces of magic plastic. For example, they might offer 90-day theft coverage from the day of purchase and double the manufacturer's warranty against part failure. Contact customer service for any credit cards you own to see if this is included.

Resetting Your NOOK Tablet

If your NOOK becomes catatonic, you can perform a Vulcan mind meld — or as Barnes & Noble puts it, a *reset.* Resets come in two flavors. One is simple and benign (and can be done any time you'd like without concern). One is much more significant. Barnes & Noble customer support may tell you to perform a soft reset or a hard reset if your tablet is acting oddly or if the battery isn't properly recharging.

Soft reset

A *soft reset* tells the device to forget any recent commands or data. It doesn't erase any of your books, documents, or configuration settings. To soft reset, do this:

1. **Press and hold the power button for 20 seconds, then release the power button.**

   That's a fairly long time. About the length of most television commercials for annoying cellphone deals.

2. **Press the power button again for 2 seconds to turn on your tablet.**

Hard reset

Performing a hard reset is significant; it forces the NOOK Tablet to clears all temporary settings. It doesn't take the tablet all the way back to factory default settings, and it doesn't erase any content. The only time you'll do a hard reset is when someone in customer service tells you to, or you want to erase your tablet before giving or reselling it to someone else.

To do a hard reset — wait, stop. Really? You sure?

1. **Press the ∩ button to display the quick nav bar.**

2. **In the quick nav bar, tap the Settings icon.**

3. **In the Device Settings section, tap Device Info.**

4. **Tap Erase & Deregister Device.**

5. **Stop. Think. Think again.**

6. **If you really, really want to do this, go to Step 7. If not, tap the Back button.**

7. **Tap the Erase & Deregister Device button.**

Fixing Wireless Weirdness

Communication without wires means you're not likely to trip over them, lose them, damage them, or otherwise object to their presence. And just as importantly, wireless communication speaks to the very essence of portability of devices like a tablet. You can download a book or a file at home or at work, and move between those two places and tap into a WiFi signal in an airport, train station, or coffee shop. I've been very few places in the world and unable to find a WiFi signal to use with my tablet (and my smartphone and sometimes my laptop computer) to connect to the web for news, e-mail (and, on some devices, to make and receive phone calls).

The NOOK Tablet doesn't currently support voice-over-Internet services like Skype or Comwave, and Barnes & Noble has indicated it probably won't go there; it wants to concentrate on things related to reading and writing.

If your wireless network isn't working properly, deal with that issue first. Here are some questions to ask:

- ✔ Is the WiFi router powered up and connected to the Internet?

- ✔ Does the laptop or personal computer "see" and communicate with the adapter?

- ✔ Is the Internet service working? Check this from the computer.

Use your computer's troubleshooting tools to check its configuration. Plus, each wireless device has a built-in configuration and setup screen you can access from your computer. Here are some possible solutions:

- Turn off your NOOK Tablet and then turn it back on. Think of it as the equivalent of clearing your head by stepping outside into the cold morning.

- Turn off the power to the router for ten seconds or so and then restore power. That may fix a problem that has cropped up in the internal memory of the router.

- Check with the network administrator to see if there's a blacklist (of blocked devices) or a whitelist (of devices that are specifically allowed entrance) for the system if you're trying to connect to a secured system (at an office or somewhere similar). You may need to provide your NOOK Tablet's MAC address (its unique identifier). To find your NOOK Tablet's MAC address, go to Settings, tap Device Info, and tap About Your NOOK. There is your MAC address. See Figure 6-3.

- If all else fails, call Customer Service at 1-800-843-2665.

I see a wireless network but can't get a good connection

WiFi networks cover a relatively small area (about the size of a small house). It may take a bit of experimentation to determine the actual working area for the WiFi system you want to use.

- Tap the network to which you want to connect, and then tap the Forget command. This erases previous settings for the connection. Then tap the same WiFi network name and see if the second time is the charm.

- Go to Settings. In the Wireless section, look at the names of networks that the NOOK Tablet has discovered. Signal strength is shown to the right of each name: one to four stacked curves. Four curves means a strong signal. One curve means a weak signal, which may fade in and out.

- Take your tablet close to the WiFi router or transmitter (7 feet away). Make sure no major pieces of metal are around to block the signal: refrigerators, file cabinets, or steel desks. (In some places, signals can be blocked by steel mesh in the walls.)

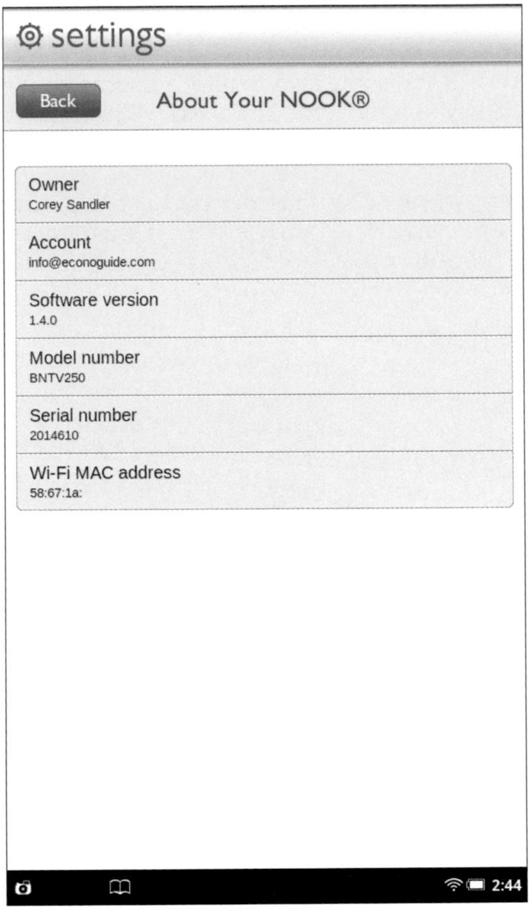

⚙ settings

Back	About Your NOOK®

Owner
Corey Sandler

Account
info@econoguide.com

Software version
1.4.0

Model number
BNTV250

Serial number
2014610

Wi-Fi MAC address
58:67:1a:

🔘 📖   🛜 🔋 2:44

Figure 6-3: Your MAC address is under Settings.

I see the network but I can't connect to it

Most wireless networks use a security system to keep unwanted outsiders from using them. You usually need a key or password, and some also require a username. You have to enter the key exactly. If the key is 6sJ7yEllowbIRD, then that is how you must enter it.

If your wireless system is at your home or office and you can't make it work with all of your devices, it might make sense to reset the WiFi router to its factory default settings and reconfigure it with all of your devices ready to be connected. Consult the instruction manual for the WiFi system to learn how to do this.

Updating the NOOK Tablet Operating System

The NOOK Tablet software may change because B&N needs to fix problems, or it wants to add new features. In most cases, the updates automatically get put on the tablet when you connect over WiFi to www.BN.com. Updating the NOOK Tablet's software should take only a few minutes and doesn't affect your Library or your Keep Reading list, and an update doesn't change the device registration to your Barnes & Noble account.

A small green ∩ symbol appears in the far left of the status bar when a new software release is available; tap the symbol to learn details about the release.

There may be some situations where a major upgrade will require a different process (such as downloading a file to your personal computer and then bringing it across to the NOOK Tablet on the USB cable). Be sure to read and follow any instructions that appear on the screen of your reader or in e-mail communications you may receive.

Knowing E-mail's Limitations

Although the NOOK Tablet's built-in e-mail application works quite well, it does have a few limitations when compared to a computer-based program (like Windows Mail) or a web-based program (like Gmail or Hotmail).

- It only displays the last 25 messages you've received. You can't use your NOOK Tablet as a portable repository of your entire lifetime's e-mail messages. That said, almost all e-mail services offer web-based access to your full account, including your extensive history of correspondence. I use the NOOK Tablet e-mail program for quick glances at the most pressing messages, and then switch over to the web when I need to go back from the future (at least 25 messages ago).

- NOOK Tablet e-mail can work with either (or both) of the two most commonly used protocols for consumer communication: POP or IMAP. That means that if you need to also read corporate e-mail from a system that's based on the Microsoft Exchange Server, you'll need to make an adaptation. B&N will be happy to sell you (for a reasonable fee) a copy of the TouchDown app, which extends the NOOK Tablet for that purpose. Check out the B&N store and search for the TouchDown app.

- The NOOK Tablet doesn't let you import or sync with your computer's Contacts list. That means you'll have to create your own list of e-mail addresses on the tablet. But you can hope for a future update that will fix that.

ISO Compatibility

You can't use just any old AC adapter and cable to recharge your NOOK Tablet; it has a pretty strong battery that makes fairly high demands on adapters and wiring. Specifically, don't use power supplies from the original NOOK or the NOOK Simple Touch.

However, the AC adapter and cable for the NOOKcolor is interchangeable with the NOOK Tablet. So, too, are most other accessories made for the NOOKcolor. (However, some NOOK Tablet accessories won't work on the NOOKcolor. When in doubt, check with B&N.)

You can also buy a car charger for your NOOK Tablet; check the accessories page of www.nook.com or your local Barnes & Noble store for availability. Please, though, don't try to read a book while driving down I-95. I might just use my smartphone to call the cops.

Don't Pay Twice, It's All Right

For people (like me) who travel a lot, one of the neatest things about the NOOK Tablet is the ability to read some of the same newspapers and magazines that are piling up on the desktop back home. But sometimes it makes you wonder why you're paying twice for the same material.

This is a problem that is still in the process of being solved, but some publishers have begun offering a discount on NOOK subscriptions to loyal customers who also have a subscription to the print version. Start by calling or e-mailing the publisher of the newspaper or magazine.

If they have seen the light and are offering a discount, it should be reflected at www.BN.com. However, you may have to do some work to introduce the bookstore to the publisher.

1. **Go to** www.BN.com **and visit My Account.**

2. **Locate the section called Manage Digital Subscriptions.**

   If the newspaper or magazine offers a discount and Barnes & Noble is aware of it, you should see a link to verify your print subscription information by entering your print subscription account number; that number is printed on the mailing label for the publication. If you have a discount but don't see it listed, call customer service and politely inquire about it.

Appy NOOK Day

The good news about the NOOK Tablet is that it can learn new tricks when you download and install small special-purpose programs called *apps,* as in *applications.* The bad news is that most of them cost money. Many app developers let you test-drive their product in a free trial.

The smart news: If a developer offers a free trial, you should take advantage. It might take only a little bit to realize that the app is perfect for your needs; then you can pay the bill and have a copy of your very own. Or you might realize that it would be a waste of money to buy the app.

Look for a button labeled Free Trial as you browse the B&N app store. And be sure you understand the limitations.

- ✓ Some free trials give you full functionality, but only for a short period of time.

- ✓ Some free trials only give limited features.

- ✓ Some free trials let you experiment with the product but don't let you save or send anything you create using it.

If you accidentally somehow downloaded and paid for an app, get yourself quickly to a phone and call B&N Customer Service at 1-800-843-2665. They just may be able to uncharge your credit card.

Getting to the Root of It

The NOOK Tablet (whose older cousin is the NOOKcolor eReader, and whose closest competitor is the Amazon Kindle Fire) and dozens of other tablets all share one important element in common: They use the Android operating system. Android was developed by the globe-gobbling guys and gals of Google.

Apple keeps the iPad's iOS operating system locked under glass (and RIM does pretty much the same with the BBX or BlackBerry 10 code for the PlayBook), but Google has been very open with its product, which is generally a good thing.

However, every developer of hardware that uses Android is free to make modifications or add a restrictive outer shell on top of the operating system. That's the situation with Barnes & Noble, which keeps a tight grip on the system within its NOOK Tablet and the NOOKcolor. If you follow all of their rules, you can only install apps that are approved by — and sold by — B&N. And you are also unable to modify the operating system or replace it with another.

That said, technology is a continual game of cat-and-mouse. For whatever reason, dozens (if not thousands) of people dedicate uncounted hours to finding chinks in the armor so they can have their way with the NOOK Tablet. The holy grail is the ability to *root* the system. This means finding a way to get at the deepest (or lowest) level of the operating system and make changes. Or the rooters may want to substitute a different version of Android with added features and no restriction on apps.

That's the place B&N would rather you not go, of course. I explain all of this because you deserve to know. But I'm not recommending that you attempt to root your system or otherwise adapt it to act in a way not endorsed by B&N. You could void your warranty.

Why? Because first of all, if you really want or need a tablet with features beyond the fairly complete set offered by Barnes & Noble, you can always buy a different device. Besides, B&N can — and has — made a number of updates to its NOOKcolor (and then for the NOOK Tablet) that have closed loopholes that hackers try to exploit.

Index

pages. *See also* web page files
animating page turns, 60
comparing, between different
versions of book, 76
dragging through quickly, 25
numbering of, described, 76
thumbnail view of, 91
turning forward or backward, 24,
76, 90, 93
Pandora app, 39, 173–174
panels, 30, 31–32
passages. *See* words
passwords
for shopping, 58, 105–106
to start or reawaken from sleep
mode, 9, 19, 55, 61–63
unsetting, 63, 106
for web browsing and social
media, 55
for websites, 151, 154
PDF files, 22, 67, 95, 140
periodicals. *See* magazines;
newspapers
personal archive. *See* archive
Photo Gallery, 36–38
photos. *See* images
phrases. *See* words
Pictures folder, 98
pinching on touchscreen, 26
Popular Lists, in NOOK
Store, 108
pop-up windows, 155
power button, 11, 27
Power Save setting, 55
PowerPoint files, 95
Pre-order badge, 131
pressing touchscreen, 22–23
previous activity, going back to, 39
privacy settings, 128–129,
151–153. *See also* security
problems, troubleshooting, 49–50,
179–180, 185–189

Project Gutenberg, 140
protected files, 66
Protection Plan, 184

• *Q* •

quick nav bar, 41–47
Quick Settings dialog box, 39–41

• *R* •

ratings of books, posting, 70
Reader settings, 60
Reading Tools, 68–74
recommendations
by Barnes & Noble, 73–74
from Netflix, 33
from NOOK Friends, 57, 131
by you, posting, 69
Recommended badge, 131
registering or deregistering NOOK
Tablet, 49–50, 104–105
repairs. *See* warranty
resetting NOOK Tablet, 185–186
Restrictions setting, 55
reviews of books, posting, 70
rooting, 119, 167, 191
rotating screen automatically,
41, 50

• *S* •

Sample badge, 131
screen. *See* touchscreen
Screen settings, 50–52
screenshots, capturing, 178–179
scrolling on touchscreen, 25
SD card, 14–16, 49, 61
SD slot, 12, 13
Search icon, 46
Search settings, 60–61

Apple & Mac

iPad 2 For Dummies,
3rd Edition
978-1-118-17679-5

iPhone 4S
For Dummies,
5th Edition
978-1-118-03671-6

iPod touch
For Dummies,
3rd Edition
978-1-118-12960-9

Mac OS X Lion
For Dummies
978-1-118-02205-4

Blogging & Social Media

CityVille
For Dummies
978-1-118-08337-6

Facebook
For Dummies,
4th Edition
978-1-118-09562-1

Mom Blogging
For Dummies
978-1-118-03843-7

Twitter
For Dummies,
2nd Edition
978-0-470-76879-2

WordPress
For Dummies,
4th Edition
978-1-118-07342-1

Business

Cash Flow
For Dummies
978-1-118-01850-7

Investing

Investing
For Dummies,
6th Edition
978-0-470-90545-6

Job Searching with
Social Media
For Dummies
978-0-470-93072-4

QuickBooks 2012
For Dummies
978-1-118-09120-3

Resumes
For Dummies,
6th Edition
978-0-470-87361-8

Starting an Etsy
Business For Dummies
978-0-470-93067-0

Cooking & Entertaining

Cooking Basics
For Dummies,
4th Edition
978-0-470-91388-8

Wine For Dummies,
4th Edition
978-0-470-04579-4

Diet & Nutrition

Kettlebells
For Dummies
978-0-470-59929-7

Nutrition
For Dummies,
5th Edition
978-0-470-93231-5

Restaurant
Calorie Counter
For Dummies,
2nd Edition
978-0-470-64405-8

Digital Photography

Digital SLR Cameras &
Photography
For Dummies,
4th Edition
978-1-118-14489-3

Digital SLR Settings
& Shortcuts
For Dummies
978-0-470-91763-3

Photoshop Elements 10
For Dummies
978-1-118-10742-3

Gardening

Gardening Basics
For Dummies
978-0-470-03749-2

Vegetable Gardening
For Dummies,
2nd Edition
978-0-470-49870-5

Green/Sustainable

Raising Chickens
For Dummies
978-0-470-46544-8

Green Cleaning
For Dummies
978 0 470 39106 8

Health

Diabetes For Dummies,
3rd Edition
978-0-470-27086-8

Food Allergies
For Dummies
978-0-470-09584-3

Living Gluten-Free
For Dummies,
2nd Edition
978-0-470-58589-4

Hobbies

Beekeeping
For Dummies,
2nd Edition
978-0-470-43065-1

Chess For Dummies,
3rd Edition
978-1-118-01695-4

Drawing
For Dummies,
2nd Edition
978-0-470-61842-4

eBay For Dummies,
7th Edition
978-1-118-09806-6

Knitting
For Dummies,
2nd Edition
978-0-470-28747-7

Language & Foreign Language

English Grammar
For Dummies,
2nd Edition
970-0-470-54664-2

French
For Dummies,
2nd Edition
978-1-118-00464-7

German
For Dummies,
2nd Edition
978-0-470-90101-4

Spanish Essentials
For Dummies
978-0-470-63751-7

Spanish
For Dummies,
2nd Edition
978-0-470-87855-2